Praise for *Make Your Brand Legendary*

"Wozniak (aka the Wizard of Woz) gives you a rare glimpse behind the curtain on how legendary brands like Chick-fil-A are launched. *Make Your Brand Legendary* is a must-read for anyone wanting to create a beloved brand."

      – **Rick Schirmer,** cofounder & chairman, Schirmer McCord Media

"If you want to transform or simply ramp up your business's success, you must read *Make Your Brand Legendary*. This step-by-step guide will be indispensable in your journey. Over the past years, we have implemented many of these tactics, and our business is thriving. It is now required reading for all new team members!"

      – **Tim Kennedy,** president, Trident Construction

"Customer experience! For-profit, as well as nonprofit corporations, create internal and external customer experiences. In *Make Your Brand Legendary*, my friend Scott Wozniak will encourage and challenge you with wisdom gained over decades of designing, developing, and delivering world-class customer experiences globally."

      – **Sam Chand,** leadership consultant, author of *Leadership Pain*

"Inspiring. Insightful. Practical. *Make Your Brand Legendary* delivers a customizable roadmap for success in any business with great stories along the way that clearly reinforces each component of the Customer Experience Engine."

      – **John Torres,** EVP of Global Leadership Development, Bank of America

"I am 100% convinced *Make Your Brand Legendary* will positively change the future for any business that follows the systems and commits to creating raving fans. I personally plan to use this book as a guide for our business to ensure we get ahead and stay ahead of our competitors for as long as I am at Trident. I can't imagine not having this knowledge and plan to recommend this book to any of my business colleagues who truly want to improve. I can't wait to see what our business looks like in a few years after we implement our Customer Experience Engine!"

      – **Todd Bulwinkle,** vice president, Trident Construction

"Absolutely game changing and mind shifting towards growth and profitability! This book will become your treasure if you are looking to build and grow a Customer Experience Engine. It gives you steps and great examples on how to create raving fans with a focus on excellence vs. success. As a businesswoman, I've learned within the last twenty-five years that customers want to do business with brands they trust and can count on. *Make Your Brand Legendary* is a perfect reflection of business insights with a personal touch of why and how. I highly recommend this book to front-line team members and executives for a high impact on any organization. I've known Scott for many years through Chick-fil-A, and he is one of the most genuine leaders I've had the privilege and honor to know and work with. I am a big supporter of his work."

– **Lana Chumachenko,** lead business consultant,
Domino's Pizza International

"Few people understand customer experience like Scott Wozniak. It's all about creating emotional connections. *Make Your Brand Legendary* shows not just what the successful systems look like, but how to build those systems that deliver consistently over time and at scale. If your organization wants emotionally engaged superfans, this is the book for you."

– **Nathan Magnuson,** founder Leadership-in-a-Box®

"In *Make Your Brand Legendary*, Wozniak's superior storytelling brings his guidance on a radical differentiation to life. His proven methods are proprietary and backed by loads of experience, examples, and verifiable outcomes. Although a book about business, *Make Your Brand Legendary* reads lucidly and practically."

– **Brian Davidson,** chief financial officer, Pepsi Cola Decatur

"Scott Wozniak's *Make Your Brand Legendary* is a treasure trove of ways to build a great company. Whether you are direct-to-consumer or business-to-business, you will find big ideas and useful advice. Plus, it's really engaging and fun to read."

– **Tony Jeary,** The RESULTS Guy™

Make Your Brand Legendary

CREATE RAVING FANS WITH THE
CUSTOMER EXPERIENCE ENGINE

Scott Wozniak

MAXWELL LEADERSHIP.

Published by Maxwell Leadership Publishing, an imprint of Forefront Books.

Distributed by Simon & Schuster.

Library of Congress Control Number: 2023912861

Print ISBN: 979-8-88710-032-6
E-book ISBN: 979-8-88710-033-3

Cover Design by Bruce Gore, Gore Studio, Inc.
Interior Design by Bill Kersey, KerseyGraphics

CONTENTS

FOREWORD

Tim Elmore

*I*n my pursuit to make the world a better place, I have learned the value of two ideals: investing in the next generation and making ideas memorable. Scott Wozniak's book, *Make Your Brand Legendary*, is a beautiful example of each of these ideals in action.

I'm excited about this book because Scott and I are both passionate about investing in the next generation of leaders. I've spent loads of my personal time and energy mentoring young leaders and creating resources for those emerging leaders. Part of the joy of investing in the next generation is seeing those leaders grow and walking with them over the years. I'm honored to say that I've been a part of Scott's leadership journey.

I first met Scott over twenty years ago when he attended a master's course that I taught on leadership and generational differences. We crossed paths again when he worked at the Chick-fil-A Support Center. He and his team helped to introduce their franchisees to my *Habitudes®* courses. For many years, we worked in parallel, running in the same circles and attending the same leadership events. He's even personally mentored some of the staff that I've hired. Over those years, Scott has grown to be a brilliant life-giving leader. His track record of impact is impressive, and he has built a reputation as an expert.

Scott's personal leadership has blessed my life, and his book has given us new ideas for improving our organization. Our relationship started with me teaching him, and now it has progressed to him teaching me. There are few things more fulfilling than that.

I've believed over the years that how you say something matters. While we need fresh ideas, for any idea to have impact, it must be presented in a way that captures the imagination and makes it come to life in the mind of the listener. Two of the best techniques for this are imagery and stories, which Scott delivers in this book. Research from 3M reminds us that visual aids improve learning by 400 percent and 90 percent of information retained is visual. Mind Tools reveals that two in every three individuals are visual learners. When you capture an idea with a vivid image, it becomes more tangible, easier to remember, and most importantly, easier to pass on to others.

I've used this principle to create leadership development tools that are used worldwide, called *Habitudes: Images That Form Leadership Habits and Attitudes®*. Big ideas delivered in brief lessons make the ideas stick. People discuss them again and again, long after the class is over. I work hard to gather the best ideas, but I work equally hard to find a visual to capture each idea.

That's what Scott did in his book. Not only does he have some truly big ideas on how to create raving fans, but he has also organized them into an overarching image, one that has depth and logic. His Customer Experience Engine sticks with people, making it easy to apply these ideas, whether for a strategic assessment or to make a specific improvement.

Make Your Brand Legendary delivers a colorful portfolio of images, from word pictures to diagrams. Scott's visuals aren't limited to just his overall frame idea. Each section of the Customer Experience Engine is loaded with imagery and analogy, helping the concepts in the book come to life.

Another key component to memorable communication is stories. Humans make sense of the world through stories. From time immemorial, people have passed on wisdom by telling stories.

It's what I'm committed to do in our work at Growing Leaders. In this book, Scott did so as well. From the beginning to the very end, you will find real stories of how leaders are implementing these ideas. It would be worth reading the book for the stories alone. With each story, the insights come to life. With each story, the ideas feel more doable. You'll be inspired, challenged, and amused. *Make Your Brand Legendary* is a wonderful example of influential communication.

Scott Wozniak is one of the rising stars in our field. I believe you should read this book for yourself, your team, and your customers. The world needs more leaders. Don't settle for

building an ordinary brand. Build a Customer Experience
Engine and become a legend.

Tim Elmore

Founder, Growing Leaders, Inc.

TimElmore.com

CHAPTER ONE

LEARNING FROM
LEGENDARY BRANDS

I want to help you build a legendary brand. What is a *legendary brand*? In each industry, you can usually find companies that stand out. If you run one of these stand-out businesses, your customers don't just buy from you; they *love* you. They buy your T-shirts and stickers so they can declare to the world that they are associated with your company. They wait in long lines to be the first to have your latest release. They drive past your competitors' locations to shop with you. They come back again and again to your store—which they probably consider *their* store—and engage with the staff like they're personal friends. Some, like Harley-Davidson's customers, even tattoo the logo on their body!

I probably don't have to work too hard to convince you that this is true. I bet you're a raving fan of someone yourself. It might be a sports team or a music group. It might be a big company or a nonprofit. It's not all of us. Some of us are more reserved and cautious with our loyalty. But a whole lot of us have a particular brand that we truly love.

Why? What is it that these legendary brands do differently from their competitors? Why do their customers love them so much?

It's not luck. Some companies have managed to do this year after year, decade after decade. It's not a fluke; it's a pattern.

I'd like you to pause right now and think of an actual example, a legendary brand that you get excited about. (If you're one of the skeptics who doesn't love any brand, then think of a brand that someone close to you is a raving fan of.) As you progress through the parts of the engine in this book, I will share my own examples to help the ideas come to life—famous ones we can all relate to and some you might never have heard of. But I want you to have your own example too. Test my ideas against your own experience to see if this actually works.

Quick note for nonprofits and mission-driven organizations: The methods in this book apply to you as well. You may have to mentally replace words like *customer experience* with *patient experience* or *client* with *member*, but whatever terms you use, this engine will get you better results, even if what you aim for isn't profit—and that's not just my optimistic guess. I know this because in addition to the business consulting I've done, I have spent many years applying these tools in a variety of nonprofit settings, from hospitals to churches to summer camps. However, to make this book more readable, I decided not to use both for-profit and nonprofit language every time I bring up a new idea. I'm just going to say things like *company* and *customer* and trust you to translate the terms in your head if it better suits your specific situation.

Whether you run a nonprofit or are a traditional business leader, whether you sell a physical product or deliver services, this book is full of practical methods for building your own Customer Experience Engine. It's not magic; it's a set of systems that work together to produce a great result. A lot of other organizations have done this, and you can too.

At this point in the discussion, I've learned that many leaders feel both hopeful and exhausted. Many of us have been told that the only way to get exceptional results is to work exceptionally hard. And if you are already tired, imagining all the extra work this is going to require can feel pretty discouraging. It's all some of us can do to keep up with the business. In fact, many of the leaders I've worked with have confided in me that leading their organizations feels like they are riding a tiger. They worry that they can't let go or the whole enterprise will spin out of control. They constantly feel a nagging pressure that they might have forgotten something important and that they're always in a tug-of-war contest with their team, pulling on the rope to keep them doing their job with excellence.

As we get started, let me reassure you. The Customer Experience Engine I will teach you to build does not require more effort than running a regular company. In fact, it is actually easier to manage a Customer Experience Engine than a company without these systems. Yes, work is required to make the shift from no engine to engine, but none of the engine systems require you to have a genius-level intellect. None of the systems require a lot of money. Each individual step is something you can do without breaking the bank or burning out. And when you put them all together, they create raving fans—customers who are easier to deal with than regular customers and who make you more money!

I have a lot of respect for the hard work you've done. But the way forward is not working harder; it's working smarter. You're already working hard. What if you could stop riding a tiger? What if you had your own Customer Experience Engine?

CHAPTER TWO

WHAT THIS ISN'T

*T*his isn't a book about how to catch a trendy wave. All the examples you will read come from companies who wowed their customers year after year. They didn't stumble into being the hottest item for a season. Instead, this is a book on how to be like Lego, whose toys top kids' Christmas wish lists year after year. It's not luck that caused Lego to grow larger than Mattel and Hasbro put together. In fact, their strong position today came after an intentional transformation. In the late twentieth century, Lego's major patents expired, reducing their toys to plastic commodities, and their sales collapsed. Why would anyone pay premium prices for their plastic bricks when their competitors sold the same buildings and characters for far less? They had to figure out how to differentiate themselves from multiple copycat companies. They did this so well that today people buy toy sets from Lego for more than twice the cost of competitor brands, without any patent protection at all.

Or consider sports fans. Teams like Manchester United (a professional soccer team in England) have hundreds of millions of raving fans around the world, far exceeding the roughly 550,000 people who live in the city of Manchester. In fact, they have 206 official Manchester United Supporters' Clubs around the world, from Brazil to Australia. Getting in street fights with fans of rival teams is far too common for some of their most unruly fans. They might love their team too much!

You might think that they have a fan base like this only because they have won a lot of championships (which they have). That can be true, but some sports teams have huge numbers of raving fans even though they haven't won a championship in years. For example, fans of the Chicago Cubs (an American baseball team) stayed fully committed to their team for one hundred and seven seasons without a championship victory. And I don't just mean they survived as a club; they survived as a wholly beloved brand.

Every year, Cubs fans walked into opening day truly believing, "This is our year!" I know this personally because

I've heard many of my own family members say this year after year. During this record-smashing losing streak, the Cubs maintained one of the best attendance figures in pro sports. In 2007, the Cubs finished second for attendance in Major League Baseball with a 97.7 percent capacity in their stadium. More astounding, they got this high fan attendance even though a large portion of Cubs home games were in the middle of the day, when people were supposed to be at work or school. Their faithfulness was rewarded in 2016, when the Cubs *finally* won a World Series championship.

Yes, winning does increase your fan base. But winning doesn't guarantee raving fans, and you can have raving fans without winning the championship. You might be thinking this is a realistic option only for big consumer brands like Apple, Disney, or Harley-Davidson Motorcycles. You might be in a more technical industry, have a business-to-business service, or find yourself price-squeezed and your product becoming commoditized. But before you give up on having raving fans, let me tell you about two of my favorite brands, Buc-ee's and Chick-fil-A.

If you're not from the state of Texas, then you might not know about Buc-ee's because, as of the release of this book, the chain has only recently been building locations outside of Texas. But if you are from Texas or the surrounding states, then you probably know what I'm about to say. I know parents whose small children ask if they can go to Buc-ee's every Saturday afternoon (no, it's not a theme park). I also personally know a globe-trotting multimillionaire who has a tradition of doing his

Christmas shopping at Buc-ee's every year (no, it's not a department store). I even know young adults who have gone there on a first date—and got a second date too (no, it's not a dance club or restaurant). Believe it or not, Buc-ee's is a *gas station* and *convenience store*. Honest. Look it up.

Like those of you who haven't been to a Buc-ee's, I was also confused when I first heard of their fans' passion for what is basically a fancy truck stop. When it comes to emotional appeal and brand loyalty, gas stations might be the lowest of the low. Sure, we realize that our cars need to refuel. We admit that sometimes we want junk food when we stop for a bathroom break during a road trip. But we expect these experiences to be dirty and cheap. They're not something we look forward to. They're a necessary evil. My motto for road trip bathroom stops has been, "Get in and get out fast, nobody gets hurt." But mature and accomplished people get truly excited when they talk about Buc-ee's. Hands start waving, eyebrows lift, breathing speeds up. They walk around with large Buc-ee's logos proudly displayed on their hats, T-shirts, coffee mugs, and even on their kids' toys. People drive out of their way, passing many other gas stations and convenience stores, to spend an entire afternoon at Buc-ee's. And this isn't happening at just one lucky location. This happens every day at dozens of locations. I'll explain how they did this later in the book, but for now my point is this: even a gas station chain has raving fans.

The other perfect example is a little chicken sandwich company based in Atlanta. Maybe you have heard of them: Chick-fil-A. If you live in the United States, you're probably a fan. And if you aren't a frequent customer of Chick-fil-A your-self, you probably know someone who is.

In fact, they've been so successful at making strong emotional connections with their customers that we probably need to pause and remember what the fast-food category was like *before* Chick-fil-A. Fast-food chains were the gas stations of the restaurant world. They were understood to be the cheapest, greasiest, rudest way to get your food. It was where you went when you couldn't afford the time or money required to get anything good.

Sadly, this is still true for many fast-food brands. But Chick-fil-A doesn't just have more sales than their competitors (on a per-store basis, it is significantly more than their competitors, often double or triple the sales per location). Every time a new location opens, hundreds of people camp out in the parking lot, sleeping in tents for two days to participate in their "First 100" party. This isn't happening just in the spring and fall or in regions with mild weather. Parking lot campouts happen in the middle of Minnesota winters and Arizona summers. I've seen entire cars professionally painted to display the Chick-fil-A logo. These customers are not satisfied with a mere bumper sticker; they want all the other drivers on the road to see that they love Chick-fil-A.

You can regularly see a Chick-fil-A restaurant with a line of cars wrapped around the building while another major fast-food chain sits right next door almost empty. I can't count the number of times someone has said to me, "I don't eat fast food... well... except for Chick-fil-A, of course."

If you can create raving fans in the fast-food and gas station industries you can create them in any category. I've personally seen this done in construction companies, enterprise software companies, accounting firms, manufacturing companies, and health-care systems. You may not have heard of them, because you're not in their category. But all the players in their niche know and love them. After more than twenty years of helping businesses build their Customer Experience Engine, I can say with confidence that there are no businesses too technical, no products too cheap, no industries too boring to benefit from a Customer Experience Engine.

You could argue that consumer technology companies have an advantage when trying to create raving fans because their products are new and exciting. But I think companies in everyday categories, like roofing and accounting, have an advantage all their own. In many of these industries, a poor customer experience is the norm. When you decide to build a Customer Experience Engine, you will stand out from the crowd that much more.

CHAPTER THREE

RAVING FANS

*O*kay, enough of the hype. Let's get specific. Raving fans are not just satisfied customers who feel good. These customers behave differently. Specifically, there are three key critical characteristics:

First, raving fans *buy more, more often*. They don't just do the minimum transaction required to get what they need; they get as much as they can, and they like the experience so much that they come back again and again. (Of course, the coming back part doesn't apply equally to all businesses. If you run a wedding chapel, for example, you probably don't want your customers coming back every year to get married. But they can add more to the wedding package or use your referral partners for post-wedding service.)

If you want this behavior, you need your customers to feel better after the experience is over than they did before buying from you. Or, to put it another way, companies with a Customer Experience Engine maximize the post-transaction feeling.

Most companies have their emotional peak at the point of sale. To put it bluntly, they want their customers to get excited enough to give them money, then they hope nothing goes wrong. That's not going to harm you, but it only creates satisfied customers, not raving fans.

Instead of measuring success by how excited they are when they say yes to the sale, you could evaluate your success by how they feel after the entire customer journey is over. You could design an experience that makes them love you more after it's all done than they did when they started.

Warning: I'm about to pick on McDonald's, and I'm going to do it several other times in this book. This could imply that I'm against McDonald's. I'm not. I grew up loving McDonald's food, and there will always be a special place in my heart for them. It was a very rare thing for me to eat at McDonald's, so

I have some cool memories there and some of their food will probably always taste like childhood to me. Besides, they're making a lot of money as a company, so I am not saying it's a failing company. In fact, McDonald's does a lot of things right. But McDonald's has built a system that's very different than the Customer Experience Engine I'm talking about, one focused on maximizing *efficiency* and *convenience* rather than on maximizing the post-transaction feeling.

For those outside the United States, you may have a very different experience of McDonald's. Its global experience is very different from the US experience. Sadly, here in the land where they were founded, the fries are cold, the staff is surly, your shoes stick to the floors, and they are really slow, despite being a fast-food restaurant built on efficiency. In America, McDonald's is widely known for their bad customer experience.

Again, they are making money. They have actually built a successful *Bare Minimum Engine* (my term, not theirs). Because of that, they are a good counterexample to a Customer Experience Engine. People often eat at McDonald's when they are hungry, in a hurry, and don't want to spend a lot of money. Plus, the idea of a Big Mac and a milkshake sounds so good when you're hungry. But after it's all done, you feel worse than you did when you first got to the restaurant.

According to multiple news outlets, McDonald's spends $1–2 billion per year on advertising and marketing media, trying to excite us enough to buy their products.[1] They spent $1.4 billion in the United States alone in 2016, according to Ad Age.[2] McDonald's is clearly making huge investments in their presale experience. Sadly, they don't work nearly as hard at making the postsale elements great. In fact, their strategy seems to be getting a sale and then doing the minimum after that moment.

But raving fans are created when you give them such a good all-around experience that they leave with the goal of coming back. It's so good they want to do more while they are with you, and they want to do it more often.

Second, if they truly love you, raving fans *pay full price*.

I'm going to oversimplify business strategy and say that there are two basic positions you can take in the market, two ways to win. You can be the cheapest option and go for lots of volume, like McDonald's or Walmart. This position requires you to enter a painful race to the bottom. You can't really stay small and do very well with this strategy, so you have to push hard to get lots of people to notice you. And in the end, the customers' loyalty isn't to you; it's to your price. If someone figures out how to offer a lower price (or is simply willing to lose money longer than you), your customers will jump ship. Your other option is to become the premium player, to offer products and services that are different and so much better than your competitors' that your customers will pay more—and say that it is worth it. In the United States, this would include brands like Chick-fil-A and Trader Joe's.

When you have customers who come more often and pay full price, you don't need as many customers as your competitors to be profitable. You can focus on winning their loyalty with a better customer experience. And when you do, your customers can't be stolen by a competitor's coupon.

A striking example of this is the many times I have seen a McDonald's across the street from a Chick-fil-A. There will be two cars in the McDonald's drive-through, while the Chick-fil-A restaurant has two lanes of cars wrapped around the building two times! All this despite the fact that Chick-fil-A sandwiches, on average, are significantly more expensive than McDonald's.

See, price isn't the whole story; value is what matters. Whether something is expensive is determined by how valuable it is to you. A $1,000 price for a granite rock the size of your fist would be really expensive. But paying $1,000 for a diamond the size of your fist would be a great deal! It's not how much it *cost*; it's how much you *get* compared to how much it cost.

Later in the book, I'm going to walk through a step-by-step plan to build a Customer Experience Engine, one that helps you become a legendary brand. Before I do, though, let me just share what you should *avoid* doing if you want to design a customer experience that helps your customers pay full price: don't discount. The more you discount, the harder it is to create raving fans.

This might sound backward to you. You might have run a coupon campaign and learned that it works—sales go up when you lower your prices.

That's actually what concerns me. Discounts work *too well*. I have learned that the more you offer discount pricing—coupons, clearance deals, limited-time offers—the more you erode your price in the mind of your customer. Every discount purchase lowers the perceived value in your customers' minds. Once they know they can buy it for less, it's harder to believe that it really is worth the original price. Sales are emotionally sticky.

If you need cash in the next ninety days, you should offer discounts. Sometimes this is the right move. When running a business, cash flow is like oxygen. It doesn't matter if a big supply of it will come to you later if you don't have enough to keep operating now. But if you have enough cash flowing to breathe easily, and if you want to maximize your perceived value, then avoid the discounts the way an astronaut would avoid cuts in a space suit.

This is harder to navigate for some of us. There are whole industries who are stuck in this trap. In America, if you order takeout or delivery pizza, you know better than to order off the regular menu. You pick your pizza only after you see what coupons or hot deals they are offering—because they are always offering discounts. And this is not limited to food. Kohl's has trained its customer to shop only when they offer 30 percent discounts in their monthly mailer and when Kohl's Cash (their rewards points) can be used. Why would customers shop at any other time? Volume discounts are standard for many manufacturing and construction companies. Even accounting firms will offer a discount if you sign up for a longer contract.

It's everywhere, and the pressure to follow the crowd in these industries is intense.

Chick-fil-A, for example, despite being in a category that is overflowing with coupons and buy-one-get-one offers, never offers discounts. Of course, you may be thinking, *Wait a minute. I have gotten a "Be My Guest" card for a free sandwich from Chick-fil-A.* That is true. They often give away cards for free food. However, giving something away for free doesn't have the same psychological effect as selling at a discount. Receiving a free item once in a while doesn't change the perceived value of the item. When you get a gift from a friend, you know the thing wasn't free. In fact, we are subtly incentivized to see it as more valuable because that increases the pleasure of receiving the gift. Free feels generous, but a discount communicates that the item's true value is the discount cost. If you want to bring in clients, offer free things as a taste test, then ask them to pay full price next time.

This doesn't work in every industry. For example, I'm not sure that a homebuilding company should give away a free house to bring in customers! (Though, if you want to experiment with a major gift like that, let me know and I'd be glad to be a test case for you.) But they could probably give away a free materials upgrade or fancy fixtures within a larger building project.

You don't have to price like everyone else in your industry— in fact, it's often better to have different pricing options than everyone else. Pricing is a story we tell, and you don't have to organize your story around being the cheapest. You can break out of the price war and get your customers to pay full price.

Price wars happen when you overfocus on beating your competitors. They happen when you feel like you have to match or beat their price. But I have learned that you can obsess about beating your competition *or* you can obsess about serving your customers. Both can drive improvement, but focusing on your competition sets the bar only as high as what everyone expects. That's why a typical doctor's office is okay making us wait and regular gas station bathrooms are nasty; they're just meeting our expectations. Legendary brands focus on *blessing their customers*, not *beating their competitors*.

Apple is a vivid example of this. Their products are among the highest-priced options in their categories, and if you point that out to their raving fans, they will proudly explain why Apple products are worth a higher price. Disney World theme parks are another example of this. The cost of taking my family there for vacation did some serious damage to my budget! Honestly, the first time I took my family I was worried that I had made a big mistake promising that to my children. But after experiencing it, my wife and I reluctantly agreed that it was worth it—and we have taken our kids there three more times since! In fact, I have taken my kids to Disney World more times than I have taken them to the Six Flags Over Georgia theme park—despite the fact that I live in Atlanta (not Orlando), and the cost of Six Flags is much lower than Disney even without travel expenses.

Note: When I refer to Disney in this book, I'm talking about the Disney World theme parks. In my experience, the other divisions of the Disney corporation don't connect with their customers like the theme parks do.

Price isn't what matters. How much value someone gets for the price is what matters.

However, before you go wild and double your prices, I should probably make at least two comments about the limits of this approach.

First, I'm not saying if you build a Customer Experience Engine, you can charge any price you want. Price always matters. Setting prices is at the heart of setting strategy. Even if your quality is better than everyone else, you still have to account for price in your competitive plan. So, don't go crazy here. If you are selling materials, like steel, or fairly common services, like lawn care, your "premium price" might be only a little bit higher than your competitors. There is a real limit on how high you can raise prices before you lose all your customers.

Second, don't be afraid to lose some customers because your price is too high. In fact, let me make a crazy challenge to you: If you aren't losing at least 5 percent of your potential customers because your price is too high, then your price is too low. If you want your service to be seen as above average in your space, then you need to be priced above average as well. Also, in my experience, in our society there are almost always at least 5 percent of people who care only about price. They are looking for the cheapest option, not the best value. If those people aren't complaining about your price, then your price is too low. Make your pricing and your messaging tell the same story.

Serious strategy and analysis should go into deciding how much to increase your prices, but a good goal is that if you raise prices 5 percent, you should lose no more than 5 percent of your customers. At first glance, that seems like you made no progress. But if you do the math, if this happened you would make 100 percent of the revenue for 95 percent of the work.

My advice is to either fix your product or fix the price. Find a price point you can sell at without needing a discount to make it a good deal. And when in doubt, don't lower your price to make it a good deal. Instead, find a way to offer things your competitors don't offer and charge a higher price.

Third, *raving fans tell others to buy from you.* Raving fans are not only valuable customers on their own but also bring you *more* raving fans. In the long term, this might be the most powerful of the three behaviors.

In modern life, we are swimming in an ocean of advertising. In 2006, J. Walker Smith (then president of the marketing firm Yankelovich) reported that the average American sees and hears over five thousand branded messages by the end of a typical workday.[3] If you think that sounds too high, pause and look around you right now. My guess is that you can see several branded images around you right now on shirts, signs, and coffee mugs. Don't forget to consider all the ads you see online or hear as you listen to music. Depending on where you are and what your daily activity looks like, you may not get a full five thousand brand impressions every day, or you might get many more than that (especially if you have a long commute to work).

All those ads blend into white noise. The only thing that always cuts through that chaos is the oldest form of marketing known to man: a recommendation from someone we trust.

We all want people to recommend our businesses, but the approach I have seen most often is to do a good job and hope our customers tell others. You have to go from *hoping* it happens to *making* it happen. You have to be willing to shift some resources from general advertising to include things that empower your raving fans to become storytellers. Just because they love you doesn't mean they're going to talk about you. You still need to give them a good reason to tell others to buy from you. You need to give them a story to tell.

See, people don't tell facts. They tell stories. So, you need to create a story-worthy moment. This requires a different kind of marketing. You should do enough general-awareness marketing so that when potential customers think of your category, you come to mind as an option. But after you reach the minimum threshold to earn some "mindshare," you can spend your time on creating experiences that inspire your core customers to tell others to buy from you.

Later in this book, I'll explain exactly how to activate your raving fans so they become storytellers on your behalf. For now, just catch the mindset shift here. I want you to shift from awareness advertising to customer activation, from broadcasting to everyone to cultivating insiders, from sharing facts to telling stories.

NOT A MOTIVATIONAL SPEECH
TO TRY HARDER

I hope it's clear by now that you don't build a Customer Experience Engine by simply trying harder or caring more. I love that you care. In fact, I'm assuming you already care, or you wouldn't be reading this book! Sadly, I've seen a lot of people who care deeply and are working hard to build something special, but they don't have any significant success to show for that effort.

If you want a different outcome, you have to build a different engine. Therefore, this book is not a motivational speech; this is not a "you should" book. It's a "how to" book.

Yes, hard work is required to do something great. But it may not be as big of a factor as you have been led to believe. In fact, when you get your Customer Experience Engine in place and running smoothly, you will probably have less stress. I've seen this time and time again. I have lived this myself in multiple leadership roles. When you have built a steady engine, you can step away from your job and not worry that it will crash without you keeping everything moving. You'll have a smooth system, a Customer Experience Engine, and its normal outcome will be raving fans.

QUESTIONS TO CONSIDER

✿ *What are the details of how an ideal raving fan of yours would behave? How much money would they spend, and how often? What price would they be willing to pay? How many new people would they bring in a year?*

✿ *How many of your current customers are raving fans (versus satisfied customers)? How many have two out of your three desired behaviors? How many have one out of three behaviors?*

✿ *How much more profitable are your current raving fans than your satisfied customers? Who is your most profitable customer (or customer group)? Who is your least profitable? (Don't forget to include the staff stress and effort required to keep up with some of your customers.)*

✿ *Who is the highest-priced competitor in your category? Who is the cheapest? How do you compare to them in quality?*

CHAPTER FOUR

BUILD AN ENGINE

*M*y first exposure to the idea of designing the customer experience was in 2003, when I was a speaker at a conference. One of the other speakers was Ken Blanchard. He talked about the ideas in his book *Raving Fans*, on stage and back in the green room. I had been a senior leader in multiple organizations by then, and his ideas on leadership, business, and even spirituality resonated with me. He described a customer relationship that I wanted to have. I went home from that conference and tried to apply his ideas to my work. This was met with some successes—but also some painful failures. I knew where I wanted to go, but I didn't know how to get there.

Then I had the chance to work inside a world-class engine, one that created raving fans on a regular basis: Chick-fil-A. For eight years, I served as a leader at the Chick-fil-A Support Center, assigned to work all over the company on strategic improvement projects. I worked directly with their top leaders, including the founder, Truett Cathy, before he passed away, and I spent my days neck-deep in a wide variety of engine parts, learning and working to help them build a better company.

Those were some truly great years. I learned a ton and I'm still close friends with many, many people in the Chick-fil-A family. But I kept getting more and more requests to help other companies, and after years of saying no, a series of small things combined to make me believe that God was calling me to step out of my comfort zone at Chick-fil-A and go back to serving other companies as a consultant. Thankfully, the first company to sign a contract with me when I announced I was leaving was Chick-fil-A, and I have continued to work with their leaders every year since then.

I had learned how to build each of the various engine components. I had seen the systems that create raving fans and had been an integral part of building them myself. So when I took my leap of faith, my question was, Will what I've learned work in another context, or did this apply only to quick-service restaurants?

The first time I attempted to build a Customer Experience Engine was for a local thrift store. It took some work to come up with a methodology that applied to them. I couldn't just tell them to copy Chick-fil-A. After teaching them my newly minted model, their sales and profits grew, and they ended up selling that store to another business. That sale delivered a much-needed chunk of cash to the nonprofit that owned it. And, yes, that thrift store is still successful today. In fact, it's the largest thrift store in the area.

Then, a credit union approached me and asked if I could help them figure out how to create remarkable member relationships. After a series of training sessions and monthly coaching with their CEO, they turned on their Customer Experience Engine. They moved from the bottom 10 percent of credit unions in their region to the top 5 percent in a little less than three years, based on industry standard measures that included return on assets (ROA), loan quality, and Net Promoter Score.

After working with the credit union, I updated my model again, using the engine metaphor for the first time.

I began sharing the diagram shown on the next page in keynote presentations. After a few years, it went from one of many topics I talk about to my most requested presentation. I received so many client requests to help with actual engine building that I put together a team of experts to work directly with these clients, each with a specialty in a different part of the engine. We've since helped leaders build their own Customer Experience Engine in a wide variety of industries, from health care to retail to churches to software start-ups. With each project,

I learned more and grew more confident that this engine really worked.

So, this book is not full of untested theories. It's not just my personal story or even the story of how one company achieved success. It's the summary of years of helping many organizations build a Customer Experience Engine. And every time I learned something, I updated the diagram, renaming a section that wasn't clear or adding a new element that turned out to be essential. In fact, the model I'm about to share is version *seven*, used by literally hundreds of companies. This is a battle-tested, highly effective strategy for building and running a legendary brand.

That's probably more than enough setup. Now it's time for the reveal. So, without further ado, here is the Customer Experience Engine:

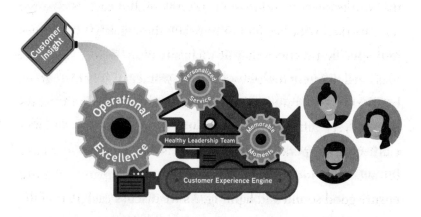

The five elements of the engine are
• Customer Insight

- Operational Excellence
- Personalized Service
- Memorable Moments
- Healthy Leadership Team

Each part is a system, a combination of tools, tactics, and teams that serve as a critical piece of the engine. Individually, they're really cool. Together, they're really powerful.

Companies who build and run a Customer Experience Engine like this don't just have satisfied customers; they create raving fans as the normal course of business.

However, before I dive into each system in the engine, there are two things I need to say.

First, you are going to need to build your own version of this engine. What I'm sharing in this book is the universal pattern that works in every industry I can think of. But each company I have worked with has had to translate these general principles into specific practices that fit their situation. Software companies need different tools to achieve Customer Insight than home builders. Restaurants will offer Personalized Service in ways that are very different than a manufacturing company. In financial services, Operational Excellence usually includes measures for accuracy and security, while a theater company works to ensure good sound and lighting. As we discuss each part of the engine, I will try to give you enough examples from a variety of companies so you can see how you can apply these ideas in your setting. But I can't cover every industry with every idea, not if

I want this to be an enjoyable book to read! So, you're going to have to do some translation work yourself. To help with that, I've included questions at the end of each chapter that should get you started strong.

For each of us, the details of our engines might differ, but the pattern is the same. These principles apply to all of us.

Second, I chose the engine metaphor very deliberately. It's not the only useful metaphor for organization building. For example, there's a lot to be said for thinking about organizational strategy like gardening. This metaphor reminds you that you can't force people to do what you want, but you can cultivate the environment so the majority of them grow in a particular direction. We see that the role of a good leader is to provide the right nutrients, protect them from pests, and prune anything that distracts from the goal. Different seasons require different strategies, and I love how this metaphor implies that the ultimate goal of leadership is to help each plant reach its full potential. This metaphor aligns really well with my worldview as a Christian and is used by a lot of the "unicorn" companies that have come out of Silicon Valley.

Succeeding in business can also be a lot like winning in sports. While growing up, I played a lot of sports at a fairly high level (I went to the state championship in three different sports and won one of them), and the sports metaphor also resonates with me—and with many, many businesses. In fact, this might be the most popular metaphor for business in America. It usually goes something like this: Success requires fitness in the fundamentals. We play like we practice, so to get better results, we should improve our practice sessions. This metaphor also forces us to face the fact that business is a competitive game. It doesn't matter that you achieved a new personal best if the other racers got to the finish line before you. If your customer experience isn't better than your competitors', it doesn't matter how hard you are working or that you're better than you were last year.

I'm also a big fan of how my friend Jim Gilmore talks about how work is actually a form of theater. That's partly because it helps you think about your business as an experience and partly because my childhood included being an actor and singer (I played a lead role in more than sixty shows, toured with a musical group, and recorded three albums, and I've worn some ridiculous costumes). Whether or not you've been a part of a show, there is value in thinking about being on stage (customer facing) versus backstage (technical support for those who are customer facing). I think all businesses would benefit from mapping out the emotional journey of a customer similar to how a stage show takes the audience on a journey. Disney Theme Parks uses this approach, for example, to the point of calling their employees cast members.

I could go on, listing other applicable analogies. Each unique metaphor can be a mental lever, opening our minds to see our lives and work in a new way. I don't think any single metaphor is sufficient to help us as business leaders. But after considering all these options (and more), I believe the engine is the best metaphor for discussing your customer experience.

Why would I pick such a mechanical metaphor for a human experience? I think defining the word will explain why. (After all, good communication begins with clearly defined terms.) *An engine is a complex machine that converts one form of energy to another using a predictable process and delivering a predictable outcome.* A complex machine is a combination of multiple machines working toward the same goal. While each process within the machine is valuable, together they achieve much more than they can in isolation. And an engine is a machine that converts energy from one form to another. An electric car engine converts electrical energy to kinetic energy (forward motion). A Customer Experience Engine converts the energy of your team into customer satisfaction.

Most importantly, a well-designed engine does this using a predictable process that delivers a predictable outcome. Far too often I see leaders talk about the quality of their customer experience like you'd talk about the weather: we can measure it and make some predictions about what's likely to happen, but we can't create it or control it. That's simply not true when it comes to customer experience. I have helped organizations go from *out of control* to *predictable* in a wide variety of organizations. And they have been able to sustain it year after year, decade after decade.

It's not magic; it's an engine. It's a stack of systems, all pointing in the same direction. It doesn't require you to have a breakthrough product. It doesn't require you to be in a "cool" industry. It doesn't require a charismatic leader.

I'm not here to hype you up. Success isn't dependent on how motivated you are. It just requires that you build five systems: Customer Insight, Operational Excellence, Personalized Service, Memorable Moments, and a Healthy Leadership Team. When you set up these predictable processes, you will get a predictable outcome. It's an engine, and every time I've seen a company operate with a Customer Experience Engine, I've seen it deliver the same result: customers who buy more, more often; pay full price; and tell others to buy from you.

CHAPTER FIVE

CUSTOMER INSIGHT

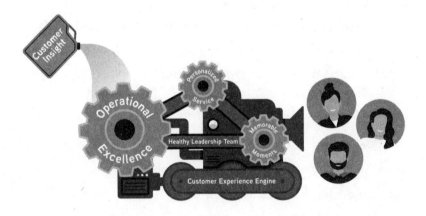

*I*t all begins with Customer Insight, which is the fuel that feeds the Customer Experience Engine.

Do you really know your customers?

I find that most organizations I work with have customer *data*, not customer *insight*. They know facts about their customers: what they buy, when they buy it, maybe even where they live or what they do for work. But they don't know why.

Why did they pick you instead of your competitors? Which of your features was the most important (and which didn't they care about)?

I'm going to play a game with you to illustrate what I mean. I'm going to describe a famous person using their public facts, and we'll see if you can guess who I'm thinking of:

- He is a white male.
- He is a British citizen who lives in the United Kingdom.
- He lives in an actual castle!
- His age is between 65–75, as of the time of this book's publication.
- He has two famous grown children.

Who do you think it is?

I've played this game with crowds in many, many live presentations, and every time, the people in the room call out the name King Charles. Each of these facts is true about him, so it's a good guess. Unfortunately, I was thinking of Ozzy Osbourne, formerly the lead vocalist of the heavy metal band Black Sabbath, who at the peak of his fame adopted the nickname "The Prince of Darkness."

These two men look alike—if you look only at the data provided. But if you go deeper than their demographics, you realize how different they really are. If you are designing an experience that would make one of these men a raving fan, you would almost certainly miss the other one. From clothes to cars, I can't think of a single product or service that they would both truly love. Maybe a castle cleaner could sell to them both? But even then, to win either of them as a raving fan, you'd probably need to present a totally different theme and use very different language when you provide the service.

Charles would probably love something called Edward Witherington III's Castle Cleaning Consultants (in business since 1645), and Ozzy would probably love a company calling itself the Vampire Cleaning Crew!

Do you know the difference between your Charlies and your Ozzys, or are you treating them all the same?

If you only want satisfied customers, a generic experience is all you need. But if you want to have raving fans, you have to get to know them better than that. You have to turn your customer *data* into customer *insight*.

As I've said, I'm here to offer practical tools, not hype you up, so this isn't an attempt to persuade you to care more about your customer. My first practical recommendation for building a Customer Insight system is to identify your customer profiles, also called customer personas, archetypes, avatars, and so on. Whatever you call it, it is a description of a stereotypical person who makes up an important part of your customer base.

For example, in the fast-food world, there is a big difference between Soccer Mom Sarah and Business Owner Beth. They both come for lunch every Monday and both buy the same meal. They're the same age and might even wear similar outfits. On the surface, they look the same. They have the same data. But Soccer Mom Sarah has two kids, one in a stroller, and is looking for a place that her kids will enjoy but is "healthy enough" for her. She loves doing DIY projects to improve her home and is volunteering in multiple causes. To win her as a fired-up customer, you can do things like carry her food to her table and put down a placemat with cartoons on it for her toddler's eating area. If there is a place for her kids to play, even better. And if she can chat with another mom or one of the staff for a little while, the grown-up conversation is a breath of fresh air for her.

But Business Owner Beth doesn't want a placemat with cartoons on her table. She feels like there is always more to do than time in the day and gladly pays contractors to do home improvement projects for her. She wants an efficient interaction with the staff but would probably rather have some space to herself to think before she has to go back into the office.

Of course, they both want good food and friendly service, but when you can articulate what else they want, you reveal how to make their experience better.

Do you know the difference between your Soccer Mom Sarahs and your Business Owner Beths? Do you have a written description of the different kinds of customers who come to you—and why they came to you?

Maybe you buy goods from one company and sell your product to another company and don't interact directly with the ultimate customers. Who is your customer? Do you focus only on the company you sell to, or do you have to get insight on your customers' customers? The correct answer is all of the above. Plus, you may need to understand the people who sell to you if there are multiple steps before you in the chain.

To create raving fans, you need to get to know each of the customers in your chain, from the first supplier all the way to the final customer. Is that a lot more work? Yep. But it's just not optional, not if you want raving fans. If each person in the chain isn't happy with what your product does, it won't be purchased again. And you may need your suppliers to adjust if you want to differentiate yourself from the rest of your market.

If possible, I recommend partnering with another company in your chain and doing this Customer Insight work together. You can shift from being one of their suppliers or vendors to a business partner. This is standard practice for many of the major players in their industry. Toyota has this kind of relationship with all their suppliers. Quality depends on everyone in the chain bringing their A game. Chick-fil-A has done this with many of their vendors, from lemon orchards to companies who provide fixtures for their restaurant kitchens. The Microsoft Office team spends a lot of time working with third-party sellers, like Staples and Office Depot, to understand and plan for how to best sell their software to the end user. And Google's Chromebook division works with schools to understand the teacher and student needs so they can better design tools for them.

So, yes, if that's your situation, you have extra work to do. Your Customer Insight won't be generated by a simple, fast process. But after doing the hard work, when you get real insight, you'll have a significant advantage over your competitors who look only at the customer right in front of them.

Most organizations never stop to figure this out. Instead, they make decisions based on their intuitive understanding of their customer. They got started by building a product or learning the skills of a service. Then they put that out in the world, and somebody bought it. So they did it again. Over the years, they may have changed the product and observed whether their customers bought more or less. They know what their customers *do*; they don't know what their customers really *want*.

You don't have to go any deeper than this if you just want satisfied customers. However, if you want lifelong, loyal customers, people who rave about you, then you need to move from data to insight.

Did you know that you can fuel a combustion engine with raw oil and it will still run? A dramatic example of this is Japan in World War II. In an attempt to put pressure on Japan to pull out of China, the United States cut off its supply of petroleum to Japan. But they still had a stockpile of raw oil. So, for a time, Japan ran engines with raw oil—including some of their battleships! It works, but it is not an efficient process. There is a lot of wasted by-product and smoke, and the engines wear out much faster. But you can create forward motion.

I've seen a lot of businesses that are run like those Japanese battleships. They are moving forward, but they're churning through their staff, creating a lot of waste and stress. You can make money this way, but it's exhausting.

Or you can refine your raw oil into high-octane petroleum. You can go from data to insight and identify what your customers really want. Then you can give them less of what they don't want and more of what they do. More motion can be generated with less effort.

But this kind of insight doesn't emerge automatically, not even if you have a lot of interactions with your customers or care a lot about them. Caring deeply about someone doesn't mean you understand them deeply—just ask any parent of a teenager! To generate Customer Insight, you have to collect good data and turn your data into insight. You need to build a Customer Insight system.

It might sound obvious to say that the first step in building a Customer Insight system is to collect data, but most companies I've seen haven't put much thought into their customer data collection. They're just doing what everyone else is doing: sending a customer satisfaction survey with twenty or twenty-five questions once a year or at the end of the project and settling for a few people who actually reply. Last time I checked, the national average response rate to customer satisfaction surveys was reported to be 3 percent. Ouch.

If that's all you're doing, you're not doing enough.

See, the better the quality of data you collect, the deeper the insights you can generate.

There are a lot of options for collecting customer data. Which of these are useful for you depends on your business. If you're a software company that sells large enterprise systems for six figures per year, your process is going to include a lot of salespeople and account managers having one-on-one conversations with the decision-makers in your client companies. But if you sell software for the general population and have millions of users, you can't collect your data primarily through one-on-one conversations. So, as we walk through what the data-collection options are, feel free to ignore a tactic that doesn't apply to you and double down on a method that fits your customer base well.

My first recommendation is to see if there is a way to collect more data as a part of your existing sales process. Start with the basic data. Find out who is buying what and how often they are buying. There is a tension between making your purchase experience as low friction as possible and collecting customer information. There's a real difference between one person buying something one hundred times and one hundred people buying something once. If you know only that you had a sale but not who made the purchase, then you don't know which of these scenarios you are in. Credit card sales provide some of that information, assuming they use the same card each time, but there may be small, easy ways to get some more information during that process, like a drop-down survey asking which feature(s) motivated their purchase. You can get demographic information about them, from age to income, or you can ask which of your competitors they considered before choosing you.

Also, if you aren't using the Net Promoter Score (where you ask your customer how likely they are to recommend you to others), then I'd strongly recommend you add this to your process too. It's one of the most validated customer data points and applies to just about every industry. You can ask this survey question in a variety of ways, from handing out cards for them to fill out, to sending out emails, to embedding codes into your receipts that they answer later.

You can have your extra question pop up after the purchase is made to avoid friction but still create an opportunity to collect the data. Or, if you are making sales in person, you can train your people to ask a question while they are ringing up the transaction or creating the contract. You can even have a graphic added to your email signature that has three clickable icons—a frowning face, neutral face, and smiling face—providing anonymous feedback in three seconds and included every time you send an email.

Bake good questions into your normal sales process. It's the most honest data you will collect. A lot of people will tell you they like your product and would consider buying it, but only some of them will actually buy it. So, when they are willing to make a purchase, you need to lean in and find out why.

Maybe this feels like obvious advice to you. But you may also be wincing a little because you aren't doing this yet. And you probably would be surprised at what isn't measured by even very successful companies. I was once hired to consult with a company on their number one priority—increasing their speed of service. It is a large chain, widely loved and highly profitable. (I won't name the company, because I don't want to make them look bad.) They are some of my favorite people and really are the best in their category by a wide margin. However, when I started the project to increase their speed of service, I discovered that they didn't measure how fast their service was—even though they had all the equipment in place to do so.

They just used their personal experience to guess how well they were doing. So, the first phase of that project was just collecting actual service times (and it wasn't what they expected). They had worked for years on various ways to improve it, but until my team and I started working with them, they didn't use real customer data when making those decisions.

Again, I don't say this to make them look bad. I share this to reveal that this is far more common than you might think. In fact, the more successful someone has been, the less they feel the need to collect data to confirm their assumptions.

And if you already have something like this in place, let me ask you a few questions: When was the last time you reviewed the questions that go on your survey? Do they reflect the priorities that you have set for your company right now? Are your questions and prompts generic (*I had a pleasant customer service interaction*) or specific and behavioral (*My customer service rep used my name when speaking to me*)?

Before you start creating a lot of new, complicated systems, there may be valuable data available for you, sitting under your nose and waiting for you to pick it up. There could be small things you can do to increase the quantity and quality of the data you collect.

Whatever you do, start small and act now. Don't let a grand vision for a robust data-collection process keep you from taking a small step this week to inject more data into your discussions. Maybe you could start by adding one question to your online sales process or have your salespeople write down one piece of info, due when they submit their sales (in this case, I recommend you make it a requirement in order for them to collect their commission).

After harvesting this low-hanging fruit, there are several advanced systems for data collection and lots of companies ready to help you get it done. You can hire outside organizations to collect data for you. This could include mystery shoppers in retail or quality inspectors in construction. You can pay for industry-trend reports from firms that analyze markets, from traffic patterns for a commercial real estate deal to consumer electronic trends. You can even hire firms to do ethnography work for you, where experts trained in studying human nature and different cultures will embed themselves into the lives of your customers, walk with them through their day, and write reports that identify your customers' deepest desires and where you fit into their lives. A lot of the biggest and best companies in the world do these ethnographic customer studies, from Coca-Cola to Honda to IBM.

There are a lot of professional firms dedicated to helping you get more data and articulate the insights. But before you do any of these expensive projects, let me suggest that you employ one of the foundational tools for collecting customer data: live observation.

You should get in the field—yes, *you*—and see your customers interact with what you sell. There's no substitute for being there in person. Walk the floors of your hospital and talk to your patients. Visit the stores and work the register for a little bit. Listen in on service calls with your staff. Stay connected to the heart of your business: your customers.

I know, you are really busy and already don't have enough time to get your tasks done, but there are big benefits to having your leadership team, even the CEO, make a habit of getting into the field.

Why is this worth adding to your already full plate? First, it's probably going to be really good for you. Most of the senior leaders I work with started in the field. Maybe that's true of you too. You were a supervisor on the jobsite or the original accountant who took care of clients. But as you grew in leadership and as your company grew, the natural consequence is to lose your connection to the *feel* of the business. The danger is that you don't realize it's happening. You still see some clients, but you used to personally interact with 50 percent of your client base each year, and now you talk to 5 percent—and they are all the older clients from the early years. You went from personally interacting with these people to reading reports about these people, and you don't realize what you're missing.

In this common scenario, you still think you know your customer, but you're using old data or believe that the 5 percent you see fully represents the rest of your customers.

I'm not saying your team is lying to you in their reports, and I'm not suggesting that you need to return to being a frontline staff member. Of course not! But I *am* saying that you used to conduct live observation of your customers as a normal part of your job, and now you are going to have to work at it. What was once automatic now needs to be intentional.

If you did not grow up in the business, then this might be even more valuable to you. All the best reports and smartest strategy discussions can't deliver the wisdom and credibility that comes from hands-on field experience. When you get out of the office and get on-site, you will learn a lot and you will earn a lot of trust from your frontline staff.

The second reason to pursue live observation is that even the best surveys have limits. Henry Ford is reported to have said, "If I had asked my customers what they wanted, they would have said a faster horse." Customers are good at describing pain points, but they aren't very good at suggesting solutions.

Insights from this kind of data collection were responsible for a huge increase in sales of Coca-Cola cans. Trained observers went to customers' homes (with their permission) to watch where and when they drank a can of Coke and noticed that the customers sometimes reached in their fridge for a Coke, only to find out they had run out of chilled cans. When that happened, they would dig into the large container of cans they had purchased and restock the fridge. They said they planned to come back for the can when it was cold. But what they actually did was drink something else and not come back until much later. Using this information, Coke changed the shape of their twelve-pack and twenty-four-pack containers so that they fit inside most fridges. They made the box longer, thinner, and even added a perforated corner that can be ripped off to give easy access to the cans. You might have a box like this in your house right now. This container was designed to go in your fridge, not next to it like the old one, so you never have to wait for a can to cool.

Customers weren't asking for a better storage system. But Coke's observation team noticed the unspoken point of frustration (in this case, warm cans when you want a drink) and offered a solution. This new box resulted in a big sales increase—all without changing the logo, flavor, or advertising.

For those who are interested in doing something like this with your customers, especially if you need to do it at a large scale or to evaluate something that isn't easily observed, then I suggest you work with professionals to at least design your approach or even do some of these visits with you or for you. You can't just show up and ask your customers to imagine a better version of your service. Questions like "What changes to our product would you like to see?" require them to see themselves objectively (most people don't) and understand which features are realistic and which aren't (that's your job). This is why Ford's customers would have asked for a faster horse. They didn't understand what a car was; they only knew they wanted to travel farther, faster.

The skill of doing these visits well is the professional discipline I mentioned earlier called ethnography. It was built on the foundations of anthropology, the study of other cultures. When it is done well, you can learn more about the customer than they realize themselves. An ethnographer working with Proctor and Gamble's product Tide laundry detergent observed a customer pour in the powder, watch the laundry machine fill with water, then reach in her hand to stir the powder into the water, requiring her to wash her hands afterward—and while she did all of this, she happily reported that the product worked perfectly and she couldn't think of a way to make the experience better. (In case you're curious, this is one of the reasons they switched from powder to liquid detergent. Both of them spread sufficiently in the water, but many customers didn't have confidence in the powder.)

If you want to get good at this, there are certification programs and firms who specialize in providing this service (including my own company). If you google the term *ethnography*, you can find several great programs to train your people on how to do this, but just because you have an expert helping you doesn't mean you should personally disengage. Every staff member of the Chick-fil-A Support Center spends at least one day a year working in a restaurant. Even the lawyers and accountants do this. And the Chick-fil-A executive team historically has spent as much as a third of each year in the field interacting with their customers and their franchisees (who are another type of customer).

No matter who is assigned to lead your Customer Insight system, the top leaders of the company need to stay connected to the customers. There's no substitute for your involvement.

As you are designing your system, I'd recommend you check out the work done by Clayton Christensen and his team around his "jobs to be done" theory. Christensen was a Harvard Business School professor who said, "People don't simply buy products or services, they 'hire' them to make progress in specific circumstances."[4] To put it simply, they don't want your stuff; they want how your stuff makes their life better.

One of my favorite applications of their work is the milkshake project Clayton and his team did. They were hired by a fast-food company to increase milkshake sales. No, that company was not Chick-fil-A, and Christensen wouldn't say who it was. I think I know who it was, and if you live in the US, you may make the same guess after you hear the story.

In America, the vast majority of milkshake sales happen in the evening. It's considered an evening dessert, consumed with dinner or enjoyed after dinner as a treat. However, this company wasn't satisfied with that. They had an asset (milkshake machine) that was largely idle all day long. So, in an attempt to increase milkshake sales, they started creating new flavors. After a lot of testing with customers, they identified a few flavors that people loved. They rolled out the product to all their locations, ran a major national ad campaign, and the customers didn't really care. Sales went up only a little—and most of them were still in the evening.

Realizing they had missed something, the company leaders brought in Clayton and his team. They didn't start with the product; they started by watching the customers. Particularly, they wanted to see the few customers who *did* buy milkshakes during the morning and afternoon. Who were they? What did they do before, during, and after the milkshake purchase? Where did it fit into their lives? What was the "job" they were "hiring" the milkshake to do?

It turned out that most of the people buying milkshakes in the afternoon were grandparents and parents buying milkshakes for their children.

The buyer was not the drinker. This insight changed everything.

See, these customers weren't "hiring" the milkshake to taste good. As surprising as it might sound, they didn't really care what flavor they got. They were hiring the milkshake to make their kids like them! (And maybe to distract them for a little bit too.) They had been saying no all day long and wanted the chance to say yes and be the hero.

I confess, I have done this for my kids. There is a Wendy's on the way home from my kids' school, and when I was the one to bring them home, they would ask if they could stop and get a Frosty (the name of their milkshake). Sometimes I said yes because I wanted to make them happy—and make them like me. Of course, sometimes I said no. Why? Because I felt bad about pumping sugar down their throats too often.

What was the brilliant solution to this customer problem? How did this Customer Insight help increase sales? Clayton and his team suggested that this restaurant company make a mini-milkshake. I can say yes to my kids while not feeling so bad about the amount of sugar I'm giving them. Flavor isn't a factor, because tasting good is not the "job" I'm hiring the milk-shake to do. The flavor had to be just good enough that my kids like it, and the original flavor was good enough for that.

By the way, sales of mini-milkshakes grew substantially, especially before dinner.

What might you learn from observing your customers in action? Do you know what "job" your customers are hiring you to do in their life? Do you know if the person who makes the purchase decision is the same person who will use your service? This separation is common for those who sell to other companies.

I've done this work enough times now that I might be able to guess what your customers want, especially if you are in a company that sells to company employees like this. If you sell directly to the CEO or owner, then there will be a lot of variety in what motivates them to say yes. But 99 percent of the time, when the person buying is not the CEO or owner of the company, they are "hiring" you to (1) make them look good to their boss and (2) make their life easier.

Do they care about your cost? Sort of. Mostly, they have a budget number their boss told them to hit. Do they care about your quality? Only if that superior quality will get them praised by their boss—and if that higher quality doesn't require extra work on their part. Do they care about your proprietary features? Well, do those features make their day-to-day work easier? Will they give them a chance to shine in front of their boss? If not, they probably don't value those extra features.

I'm not saying they don't want their company to succeed or their owners to see more profits. I'm saying that all those considerations are filtered through this lens: (1) Will this make me look good to my boss? and (2) Will this make my life easier?

This insight can be used in all sorts of ways to make your stuff more valuable to customers. Can you simplify how they interface with you so they get the same results with less effort? What if you sent them an unbranded presentation on the changing trends of the market—encouraging them to share it with anyone they want? This allows them to say, "Hey, boss, check out what I've been learning."

My team has been consulting with a company for several years, and they recently asked us to work with one of their markets in Texas to transform the customer experience. The regional leader, who was our partner on the project, did a great job leading his people, and we had a great time working with him. With this in mind, I sent an email to the boss of the regional leader (the national brand leader) and copied him, saying, "Brady, I just wanted you to know that Mike is doing a phenomenal job." I listed some of the specific things Mike had done well and thanked Brady for developing such a great leader. My original plan was to send this email to Mike, and only at the last minute did I remember to apply what we teach.

Better insights allowed me to be more effective without more effort.

What data are you collecting? The quality of your insights depends on the quality of your data. Before trying to guess more intelligently, maybe you should go upstream and get more and better customer data.

However, data points alone are not enough. In fact, it can actually be bad for your company if you jump from a data point to action every time. Not all the feedback you get will be useful. Sometimes, people who are not your target audience will tell you specific things to make your service better—but you shouldn't do what they suggest. If you are making something trendy for teenagers, you don't want to ask their parents what the kids think is cool.

I usually advocate for faster decision-making in companies. But when doing Customer Insight work, I actually encourage leaders to put a small process in between data and action. You don't have to make it complicated, and it doesn't require special skills, but a little time to stop and think could save you a lot of time. In fact, there are just three fundamentals to a good insight process: repetition, questions, and patterns.

First, repetition is vital. Though this might sound obvious, you need to do this work on a regular basis. Sure, it's possible that you will experience a eureka moment if you do this once. Rather than hoping you get lucky, though, you can build an engine, an ongoing system of Customer Insight with repeatable actions that make you a little better each time. Plus, over the years, your customers will change as the world changes around them. Repetition allows you to change how you serve them in real time.

Let me pause and do a quick reality check with you: When in your calendar do you have time blocked out to look at customer data? Who will be joining you for that discussion? How often will you do this? I recommend you do this at least twice a year, and more often if you're in a volatile situation. Make time to sit down for an hour or two and dig into your customer data to look for insights on what they truly want.

Second, ask honest questions. The better your questions, the better your answers will be, so craft good questions. The exact questions will change based on your unique situations, but there are some universal questions that you can start with as you craft your own:

- Who are the people that buy from us?
- Are there common traits between some of them?
- What archetypes or avatars can we name?
- What was happening in our customers' lives before purchasing from us that made them feel like they needed what we offered?
- Who else did they consider buying from?
- Were there any differences between their expectations and what we delivered?
- How did they actually use our product/service?
- Did they do anything differently than we expected?

When you ask your questions, it's absolutely critical that you adopt a beginner's mind. Beginners ask obvious questions and change their mind easily when new information is presented. They have no ego to defend and nothing to prove. Without that kind of humility, you might spend time on this and yet learn nothing. If you believe you already know everything you need to know, you will either miss or dismiss any data that challenge the way you currently think.

The smarter and more experienced you are, the more tempting it is to close off your mind to new ideas. But it's not automatically true that experts can't learn like beginners. It is possible to have the best of both worlds. Perhaps the ultimate example of this is Kano Jigoro. He was a black belt in multiple martial art disciplines and even invented the martial art judo. As an old man, he told his students, "Bury me in my white belt." Instead of choosing any of his earned black belts, he chose the belt of the total beginner. He was prouder of his ability to learn than of all his formal titles.

With that in mind, let me add one more question to your insight process: What are you sure of about your customers—so sure that you haven't checked in a long while to see if it's still true? After taking an honest look at the data, you may return to most of your original conclusions. But you will never know which of your assumptions is no longer true until you test them.

Third, while you are asking honest questions, look for patterns. Look for repeated words and correlations between things like sales and seasons of the year. If you worry that you'll find yourself sitting around a room with your team looking at spreadsheets and wondering where the patterns are hiding, then you can get help from someone who specializes in this work. There are tons of methods to guide a team from disorganized data to actionable insight.

Many larger companies have a team on staff dedicated to researching customer trends for their industry, gathering all their latest customer survey info, monitoring social media chatter about their company, and compiling that (and more) into a Customer Insight report. The Chick-fil-A Support Center produces a report like this monthly, titled "Voice of the Customer." In fact, since all their restaurants are franchised, they create an insight report on their franchisees too.

If you have a large data set, you may want to have someone help you with data science tools or even apply AI software to help you find nonobvious patterns. But you can also do a lot with human ingenuity too. For example, you might notice that although the specific words in the customer comments are different, there is a theme of feeling safe and secure. When done well, this process is a fusion of art and science.

When doing all this analysis, keep in mind that your first goal is to document clear and compelling descriptions of your customers' personas, their external traits, and their internal motivations. After you have established insights on who your customers are and what they want, keep searching. As you grow, the goal is not to confirm what you already believe; it is to look for deviations from the pattern to find the outliers that don't fit your expectations. When you find them, savor the surprises. These are often the most valuable discoveries.

Earlier, I dismissed customer surveys as ineffective. But the truth is, I'm not down on surveys; I'm down on the way most people send their surveys. There is a low-effort, high-return way of using customer surveys to improve your Customer Insight system: pulse surveys.

Begin by splitting up your survey of twenty-five to thirty questions into a series of mini-surveys, each with a few questions, four at the very most. Instead of sending all the questions at the end of the year (or the end of your project), send out these pulses throughout the life of the project, maybe once a month if you have an ongoing customer relationship.

You probably get surveys from companies all the time. I do. Do you answer all of them that are sent to you? I don't. Why not? Primarily because I don't have the time for that. But when I know it's just a few questions, I'm much more likely to pause and take care of it. You need to make it very clear when you send it out that you have only two or three questions. And you can't cheat by making them multipart questions or require an essay from them. My recommendation is to use rating questions, on a scale of 1 to 5 or 1 to 10, with an optional comment box.

The goal is to make something they can do in thirty seconds or less.

That's the first improvement of a pulse survey. By lowering the time required to respond, you will increase the percentage of those who answer.

But don't stop there.

I don't answer many customer surveys, but sometimes I do—and I have never received a real response. Sure, I got the form letter. ("Thank you for taking our survey. Your input is important to us.") But that doesn't count. I finally spent my time to help them, and what did I experience? Nothing. It's like throwing my input into a black hole and hoping someone on the other side will do something with it.

What if you actually responded to your customer surveys?

You could send an email to everyone, saying something like, "Thank you, those of you who answered. Here is one big idea we got from what you said." Or even something as simple as, "We realize we need to change this part of our service. We don't know how we will do that yet, but we are working on it and are so glad you let us know."

When you do this, your survey will go from requiring a lot of time from them while delivering no value to being something that takes little effort and gets a reply. People begin to think, "This company is listening to me. My voice is making a difference." For some people, this is enough to change your survey experience from a negative to a positive.

If I stop here, this will be really good for your customer—and not so good for you. If you do this you will increase your workload by 2,400 percent! You could go from annual survey responses you didn't have to answer to sending twelve surveys a year plus twelve replies a year. It might still be worth it, but there is one more recommendation I have as you build this system: turn this into a leadership development program in your company.

This work is important, but it doesn't require the CEO to do all the tasks. You can give this to a rising rock star in your company as a special assignment. It doesn't have to be a promotion or a pay raise, and it's not permanent. You can tell them you've seen potential in them and ask them to take this on for the next twelve months. Then, you just give them the questions for them to send out each month.

I suggest spending fifteen minutes each month in your leadership team meeting to discuss your pulse survey. This gives your rising rock star the chance to join that meeting, share the results, and discuss the reply you want to send.

They get face time with your leadership team and get to know your customers really well. You get to discuss customer data regularly without having to do the tactical work to collect it.

Your customers will love it, your leader will grow, and you will have a true Customer Insight system running.

Do you see the difference between this ongoing dialogue created by your pulse survey and sending the annual survey and hoping you remember to do something with the few results you get?

You don't have to hope insight comes to you. You can build an engine and make this a part of your normal operations.

As you read the rest of this book, if you ever feel like you don't know which option is right for you, please do not guess. Instead, go upstream and get more Customer Insight.

That's why I depict Customer Insight as the fuel for the Customer Experience Engine. To oversimplify business, you provide something customers want enough to pay for. To be successful, you must understand what they want.

And when you move from raw data to real insight, every other decision gets easier. The investment in this system will pay off in a big way. You will save so much time and money by knowing your customers. Every choice you make should be run through this filter: What do your customers truly want? What job are they hiring you to do in their lives?

QUESTIONS TO CONSIDER

✿ *When, in your calendar, do you have time blocked out to look at customer data and ask good questions about it?*

✿ *Who will be joining you for that discussion?*

✿ *What about your customers are you sure of—so sure that you haven't checked in a long while to see if it's still true?*

✿ *Who are your core customers? What else can you find out about their life in addition to how they use their product?*

✿ *Who is not your customer? Who should you feel free to say no to as a customer? Are there any customers you should considering "firing"?*

✿ *What is a good cadence for your pulse surveys? Monthly? Bimonthly? Project based?*

✿ *When customers take your surveys, do you respond with what you've learned from them?*

✿ *Who could serve as the temporary leader of your pulse survey?*

CHAPTER SIX

OPERATIONAL EXCELLENCE

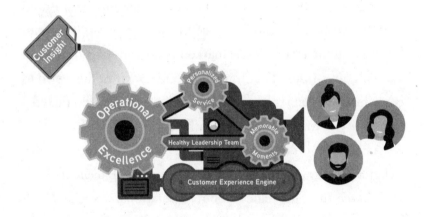

*C*ustomer Insight is critical, but it's not customer facing. It informs what we do for our customers, but insight alone doesn't serve your customers. It's a tool for you, not for them. So now we turn the conversation to focus on crafting the experience of the customer. There are three gears at the heart of the

engine, three systems that define what your customers experience. The first of these is Operational Excellence.

This is not what most people expect me to talk about. This
is a book about how to wow customers, right? Shouldn't we be
talking about sending handwritten notes and gift baskets? We'll
cover that, but not yet. While those matter, they aren't where
we start.

So, where *do* we start? We start with Operational Excellence.

Operational Excellence is first in sequence and first in
priority. If you don't get this right, nothing else matters. In fact,
let me give you the "Scott Wozniak Plan for Driving Your Brand
into the Ground." If you hired me to ruin your brand, I would
help you build a world-class marketing and advertising system
and bad operations. That way, we would convince the world to
come find out that you are bad at your job and they can then tell
everyone else to avoid working with you.

Assuming you don't want to destroy your brand, you have
to figure out how to show up with Operational Excellence.

There's nothing fancy about Operational Excellence. It
includes basics like the food served hot, the software not
crashing, the financial details being captured correctly, and
your staff providing friendly service. After you get good at these
fundamentals, you can explore ways to offer services none of
your competitors offer. But first you have to earn that right by
becoming excellent at the basics.

Before I talk about how to do this, I want to make sure we
are on the same page. See, when I talk about excellence, the
human instinct (mine included) is to think about our best day.

We want to think about what it's like when everything goes right. We think about how smart our staff can be or how fast our tools are. We equate our excellence with our skill level.

But your customers are not asking how skilled you are. The question your customers are asking is, "Can I trust you?" If I give you my time and money, can I trust you to deliver what I need every time?

One of the best illustrations of the power of this principle is McDonald's food. Earlier in this book, I claimed that their french fries are cold. If I'm being honest, though, that isn't always true. On rare occasions, I have walked into a McDonald's and caught them when the fries came out of the frier, and those fries were good! Seriously, no offense to my good friends at Chick-fil-A, but McDonald's might have the best french fries in the business—when they are fresh.

The problem is not that I have never had great fries at McDonald's. The problem is that I have also gotten them after the fries have been sitting under the warming lamp for thirty minutes and have become tough, cool, and chewy.

The hard truth is that being inconsistently excellent will earn you the same amount of trust as being consistently bad.

It doesn't matter if your fries are good some of the time. If I don't trust them to be good consistently, I won't drive there to buy them.

Another example is the McDonald's ice cream machine. When I give presentations and mention McDonald's ice cream machines, every single time someone shouts out, "They're always broken!" before I can say anything further. All over the country, people are upset about the ice cream machines. It got so bad that an angry customer created a website to track how many of their ice cream machines were broken: www.McBroken.com.

No, that's not a joke! In fact, I recommend you pause and check it out right now.

If I understand this correctly, the developer of this website began with the Google Maps tool and has the software to order an ice cream cone from each McDonald's location. If a store returns the message that the product is unavailable, the pin for that location changes on the map from green (working) to red (broken). On this site, you can zoom in to your city, zoom out to your state, or even check the whole country. (There are a lot of red pins!)

McDonald's hates this, of course. Not only is this horrible for their reputation, but I'm told it also feels unfair. The public belief is that they are always broken, even after viewing this site. But when you look at the actual data, you might be surprised by the percentage of broken machines.

I've checked this site many times over the past few years as an interactive part of workshops I have led for clients, and the national percentage of broken ice cream machines has ranged from 10 percent to 14 percent, with 11 percent being the most common. While writing this paragraph, I just checked again, and the McBroken website reported 10.63 percent of broken ice cream machines in the United States.

That means almost 90 percent of the McDonald's ice cream machines are working. That's a long way from all of them always being broken. What's going on here? Are we just being unfair to McDonald's? Is this a false rumor?

It is easier to share negative stories than positive ones, and a bad reputation is hard to change. What this site tells me is that 90 percent excellence isn't enough to earn your customers' trust. Remember, inconsistent excellence earns the same trust as being consistently bad.

Your customers don't give you credit for your best day; they judge you by your worst day. They aren't asking how skilled you are; they are asking, "Can I trust you?"

The core of Operational Excellence is *consistency*. Only consistent excellence counts.

At this point, in my experience, you may have gotten fired up about this and are imagining the motivational speech you will give your team. You might even be planning to use the McDonald's illustration I just shared. That's a fun story to share, and I'm all for it. But before you run too far down that road, I have good news and bad news.

The bad news is that your motivational speech isn't going to work.

You don't build a strong system of Operational Excellence by being charismatic and inspiring. If you're a good communicator and speak with passion to your team, you can increase their performance for a month, maybe two, but at some point, they will get tired and go back to the engine you built.

Edwards Deming said it well: "Every system is perfectly designed to get the results it gets." If you have a part of your business with inconsistent excellence, congratulations. That's the system you have built. And no amount of motivational speaking will change that.

Leaders who try to create Operational Excellence through motivation alone remind me of the old joke of bad leadership, "The beatings will continue until morale improves."

However, this is also the good news.

If you want different outcomes, you can just build a different engine. You don't have to be a great speaker or a charismatic leader. You can make systemic changes that will improve your Operational Excellence whether you are whipping your team into shape or not.

One of my personal favorite examples of this comes from the Disney World Theme Parks. Most of my childhood was spent in Florida. I grew up loving Disney World, and I'm not alone in my appreciation for those magical playgrounds. Orlando, Florida, the home of Disney World Theme Parks, receives more vacation travelers than any city in the world, in large part because of Disney World. There are other theme parks all over the world, but no one else even comes close to Disney's parks, measured just about any way you choose.

Many factors go into making the Disney magic happen. They have built a Customer Experience Engine just like I'm describing in this book (though they use different wording). It's so good my company even leads retreats to Disney World to study how they do it. And while we are there, we point out to the participants that one of the most remarkable factors in their magical experience is something you *don't* see: trash. With over a million guests per park (on a slow day!), there is a lot of trash to deal with. But next time you're there, look around and see if you can find a single piece of trash on the ground. And if you do find one, keep your eye on it and see how quickly someone comes along to sweep it up.

Cleanliness is one of Disney's Operational Excellence fundamentals. Rather than rely on motivation, Disney has built a system to ensure they have cleanliness all day, every day. Some of the success can be attributed to hard work. There are more than 120,000 Disney employees dedicated to upkeep at all the Orlando parks and resorts. But they don't rely on pure labor alone. They have done their own research and set up a robust system of cleanliness. Specifically, they did a study to see how far away a trash can could be before a guest would feel like it was *too far* and instead just "accidentally" drop their trash at their feet. The answer was twenty-seven feet. (For the record, I'm not sure I like what that says about humanity!) They could have complained about the sloppy habits. They could have put up "Don't Mess with Disney!" signs to motivate people to be more thoughtful. They could have added this to all the safety messages around the park. But instead of trying to achieve excellence through motivation, they installed more trash cans. In fact, wherever you are in a Disney Theme Park (unless you are in a queue for a ride), you are never more than twenty-six feet away from a trash can.

I can personally confirm that this systemic approach works. I've not only verified this at multiple Disney theme parks but have also installed this system in my house. I have four children, and like all children, they generate a lot of trash. My wife and I have lectured them on cleanliness a lot, but after learning about the Disney system for trash management, I decided to change my approach at home. I bought more trash cans and placed them all throughout my house. There are two entrances to our kitchen, and we had one large trash can; now, we have one large one at each entrance. I placed trash cans next to every nightstand and also near every door in my children's bedrooms.

We have three small trash cans in our living room alone, all discreetly in arm's reach so that my kids don't even have to walk to the other side of the room to throw things away.

You could just get upset when you see trash lying around, or you can build a system to make cleaning easier.

Again, I'm not interested in just getting you hyped up; I want to talk about how to build your engine. I will share eight *levers* you can pull to increase your Operational Excellence. You may have more options that are unique to your industry, but in my years of helping companies build their engines, I have found these eight levers work in just about every industry.

LEVER 1:
HIRE WITH EXCELLENCE

The first lever is by far the most important one. If you want Operational Excellence, you have to hire with excellence.

It doesn't matter how smart your systems are, how efficient your tools are, or how much pressure you put on your team to perform. If you don't have the right people in the right roles, you won't achieve Operational Excellence. As the old saying goes, you can lead a horse to water, but you can't make it drink. If you put great people in a sloppy system, they will find a way to make things work with excellence. But if you put the wrong people in a smart system, they will find a way to do the least amount of work possible. It surprises me how creative and diligent people can be while working to avoid work!

When I talk about hiring, I specifically mean recruiting, selection, and onboarding—the process of bringing people from outside your organization into your team and making them fully functioning staff members. This topic deserves an entire book, but I will highlight a few factors to illustrate what a strong hiring process looks like.

Let's start with recruiting. I had the chance to participate in a $1.5 million project to study how to recruit quality staff. We put an extra emphasis on skilled hourly labor since most of the research we could find focused on white-collar office labor. We learned a lot. Some of our work confirmed what other studies showed, but other findings were new to us.

For example, we discovered that paying higher wages than your competitors only attracted more low-quality employees. Don't get me wrong; nobody complained when they were offered more money. But the high performers we wanted to attract cared much more about other factors, such as whether the job would give them a chance to learn more skills, whether they had friends who already worked there, and if the organization had a noble mission or purpose they could get excited about. The way you recruit and what you choose to emphasize in your job postings attract different candidates to apply.

I've also found that most people don't put nearly enough thought and effort into their selection process. They spend time and money getting several candidates to interview, then a variety of people talk to each candidate and share their impression with each other. But there isn't a clear list of things to look for—or to watch out for. There isn't a scorecard to capture how well a candidate did in each of the important areas. And there isn't even an attempt to have all the interviewers ask similar questions, so you can't make apples-to-apples comparisons. The best hiring processes don't rely on the judgment of seasoned people. They have a system.

For example, many great organizations I have worked with look for the "three Cs" in their interview process: character, chemistry, and competence. Character isn't just being a nice person; it's about the unique wiring and values of the person you are interviewing. Again, not everyone is a good fit for your organization's values. I'm not talking about a generic personality stereotype like whether someone is an introvert or extrovert. I'm talking about deeper values that make some of your work fun and other types of work frustrating. Some organizations need people who are passionate about precision and love to execute a process one thousand times in a row, making it a little better each time. And other organizations need people who love to try new methods and get nauseous at the idea of doing anything repeatedly. Some jobs are a good fit for people with natural focus who will put their heads down and work on making things on their own. Other jobs are a better fit for people who thrive on managing the chaos of constantly changing customer requests.

Do you know what character qualities your entire company is looking for? Do you know what character qualities would be best for the different jobs in your company? And do you spend part of your interview process evaluating whether they have the character qualities you are looking for?

You can't just ask if they are a hard worker. (Everyone will say yes.) But there are questions you can ask that will reveal whether someone has the character qualities you want. If you are looking for people with a lot of self-driven determination, you can ask them about a project they kept working on even when others told them they should quit. If they don't have a story like that, they might not be that kind of person. Or you can test for their learner's mindset by asking about a project that went wrong. How they handled that failure in the moment and how they describe that experience to you can reveal a lot about their teachable spirit. Don't *hope* they have good character; look for signals from their history to indicate they already have these qualities in their lives.

When I speak about selecting people with the right character, a question often comes up about whether you can *change* someone's character. There's a lot of debate on this, with people firmly entrenched on each side of the question. As a Christian, the answer is pretty clear to me: yes, people can change character. Character change is central to the Christian message (believing in Jesus and following Him results in a changed heart). But I don't think you should hire someone whose character doesn't *already* match your organization's values.

Can you change their character? Sure. But it's a lot of work. It's hard, exhausting, unpredictable, and takes a long time. In fact, we have all experienced the process of character change. Most of us just call it parenting. We begin with an adorable little narcissist and try to turn them into someone who serves others, plans ahead, and follows basic hygiene. It's challenging, exhausting, unpredictable, and takes eighteen years—at least!

So, yes, I'm a big believer in character change. I have seen my own character change in major ways throughout my life, and I am continually working on growing my character even more. But I don't think it's a wise use of your company's time and energy to try to change the character of your employees.

Let other organizations, whose purpose is to help people change their hearts, do that work. You can even give time and money to support your favorite character-changing organizations, from churches to orphanages. And you should hire people who already have your character qualities in full measure.

The second of the three Cs, chemistry, is about their people skills. They don't all need to be extroverts or eloquent speakers, but they should all be people you enjoy spending time with. Whether we like each other greatly affects how we work together. If I see you about to make a big mistake, but I don't know you well or, worse, don't like you, it will affect the way I approach you about that mistake. I may not even say anything. But if you are someone I like, then I am much more likely to pull you aside to talk about it or even put in extra time to help you fix it.

An employee's ability to connect with others and interact in healthy ways will determine whether they will receive feedback and improve or get defensive. It will affect whether your teams work well with each other or if silos form in your company. And the higher up in leadership, the more central people skills are to being effective. Plus, many of us will spend most of our days with our coworkers. We don't have to be best friends, but who wants to spend this huge percentage of our lives with people we don't like?

Don't *assume* chemistry is going to be good. Test for it. It could be as simple as asking them to eat lunch with you and the rest of the team they will be working with. It could be asking them to spend time on the jobsite, interacting with the staff they might lead. Whatever your method, make sure a chemistry check is a part of your interview process.

The third of the three Cs is competence. This is the only thing most companies look for in their interview process, so I don't feel the need to spell out all the ways to evaluate competence, from résumé validation to observing them doing the work of their job. Competence is essential, but if I can't find a *perfect* candidate, then the only category for which I am willing to accept a less-than-perfect fit is in their competence. Character is hard to change, and chemistry skills take a long time to learn. However, you can teach new hires competency as long as the other two Cs are strong.

If all of this seems like a lot of work, you're right. Evaluating all of these takes more than one interview. This not only requires more thought but also requires you to invest more time.

For example, the average number of interviews required to get a first-time job at a Chick-fil-A restaurant (a teenager who will work the cash register) is more than most of their competitors. It requires three interviews. For comparison, the average McDonald's doesn't require a face-to-face interview at all, just an acceptable job application. (Note: the specific practices will vary from location to location in both of these chains because staffing decisions are handled by the local franchise owners, not decided by the franchisee headquarters.) When I got hired to work at the Chick-fil-A Support Center in Atlanta, I went through seventeen interviews before they offered me the job.

To be clear, the goal is not to conduct a lot of interviews. During my time as a staff member at Chick-fil-A, we worked hard to make the process more efficient. But while we shortened the process, we never figured out how to get clarity on a candidate's job fit with only one interview. I don't think it's possible.

You may be getting concerned right now, thinking, *I don't have time to do all this work! I already have too much to do and need to hire someone fast.* Well, I'm sorry to say this, but you don't really have a choice. Either you will spend time on hiring with excellence or you will spend time managing misfit employees who aren't meeting your Operational Excellence standards. (And it usually takes a lot more time to manage misfit employees.)

For a short while, you may have to put in extra time to upgrade your hiring process while you manage the team you have, but step-by-step, your high-quality hires will reduce your need to monitor and motivate your team at very high levels.

Let me share my nonscientific test to determine if you need to upgrade your hiring—a gut check, if you will. If you feel like you have to play tug-of-war with your team and constantly pull on the rope to keep them engaged and working hard, then you need to upgrade your hiring process. Your team shouldn't need you to constantly pull them back to the work, not if they have all three Cs. Your team should be on the same side of the rope as you are, pulling *with* you against your competition and toward your goals.

You will still need to lead them to ensure everyone is pulling in the same direction. But as my mentor, Jimmy Collins, taught me, I'd much rather restrain a mustang than kick a mule.

Legendary brands have legendary people. At the end of the day, everything else assumes you have the right people in the right roles. When I'm consulting with companies, roughly 75 percent of the time my team and I discover that their sloppy operations are actually evidence of sloppy hiring finally showing up.

If you want Operational Excellence, hire with excellence.

LEVER 2:
PUT A LEADER ON IT

While hiring the right people is the single biggest factor, it's not enough to drive consistent excellence by itself. Even if you have great people, some work will slip through the cracks. It will get done some months and left undone other months. When this happens, the way to solve this is to put a leader on it.

The sad truth is that the best way to starve a dog is to assign five people to feed it. When no one owns the responsibility for feeding the dog, everyone assumes someone else will do it.

Sometimes the reason you have inconsistent excellence is because it's not a top priority for anyone in your organization. It's on their list, but it's not on the top of the list. Tasks like these get done when we have leftover time—and some months, there isn't any spare time.

A classic example of this is safety in a construction company or manufacturing plant. If safety is everyone's job but no one is responsible for monitoring or maintaining the safety standards, then compliance will be inconsistent. I've seen this change over-night when someone was named the safety champion. It's not that your employees changed their minds about safety over-night. (I have never seen a company where people wanted to be unsafe at work.) It's just that it wasn't their top priority.

Oh, and the worst person to carry a responsibility like this is the CEO. They might care deeply about the project, but they have the whole company on their plate. They of all people are the most likely to get pulled away to deal with urgent issues like a cranky customer or a staff crisis. CEOs need to stay aware of all the important processes of their company, but the bigger the company gets, the less likely they can be effective as the leader who creates consistent excellence. In this case, you might need to put *another* leader on it.

Some projects are so big and important that you may need to hire someone full time to lead them, but some of these can be part-time projects or even just a special assignment that doesn't require a new title. Remember my recommendation for the pulse survey? I suggested giving responsibility for your pulse surveys to a rising rock star. That's a good example of this principle in practice. They will care more about that Customer Insight work than the CEO because it would be one of thirty-nine things on the CEO's plate, but it would be one of the top three things on that rising leader's plate.

If you have inconsistent excellence in some part of your business, maybe you need to name someone to lead it. Everything improves when you put a leader on it.

LEVER 3:
DEFINE IT

Another source for sloppy operations is sloppy language. *Excellence* might be one of the most dangerous words in business. Leaders will say that word, their people will say it back, and everyone will think they are in agreement. But it turns out that each person means a different thing when they say that word.

It's a bit like how my kids and I use the word *clean*. Over the years, I have had my children come to me with complete sincerity and tell me that their room is clean. They believed it. But when I checked, I discovered that their definition of the word *clean* is not my definition.

Your people might be sincere in committing themselves to excellence, but without a clear definition of what that means, they could be delivering different services than you envision when you think of excellence.

Disney Theme Parks don't just tell their staff members to be hospitable to the park guests; they give them specific things to say and even define precisely how to point when giving directions (using the whole hand and not a single finger). They don't hope their staff knows what excellent service looks like; they spell it out for them.

Another example of this is how Chick-fil-A talks about friendly service. Many companies tell their people to be friendly, but Chick-fil-A has defined four service behaviors (the Core Four). Rather than assume a nineteen-year-old knows what it means to be warm and friendly, they explain it to them. The Core Four service behaviors are

1. Make eye contact
2. Share a smile
3. Greet them enthusiastically
4. Always say, "My pleasure!"

Some brands will put new staff members in front of customers, then come back and tell them they weren't friendly enough—only to have the teenager argue with them. But you can't argue about these behaviors. You can pull out your phone and record someone working a register, for example, and if they don't make eye contact, you can show them the recording.

This kind of clarity on excellence even elevates the way you hire. I bet you can guess what behaviors the Chick-fil-A franchise owners look for when conducting their three interviews.

You can hire random people and try to train them to smile, or you can hire people who smile in all three interviews. As a bonus, you can pat yourself on the back for your brilliant training skills when they smile all the time. And in private moments, you can admit they would smile anyway!

This applies to more than service interactions. One of my favorite applications of this level of clarity is management by picture. Setting up a workspace with tools is fundamental for staff excellence in all sorts of fields, including manufacturing, commercial kitchen, construction, fabrication shops, and even operating rooms. Set up the location exactly as it should be, take a picture of it, then print, laminate, and hang that picture on the wall over the workspace. Instead of talking about it vaguely, point to the image and tell them they did a good job when it looks exactly like the picture. It's easier for the employee to know what they're supposed to do, and it's easy for a manager to evaluate if they did it correctly. It also avoids an opinion battle over whether a space is clean enough or their tools are organized correctly.

If you haven't already done this, I strongly recommend you sit down with your leadership team and create a list of your Operational Excellence fundamentals. It might be interesting to have everyone write their own list and then compare and discuss it until you all agree on the core list. In general, I have found a complete list has six fundamentals at most. If you have too many items, you might be talking about multiple product categories or business units. Each of those will need to have its own list of fundamentals to get right.

The more specific your list of excellence elements, the better. These will be very different for each company. If you run a restaurant, your list will probably include things like the speed of service, the taste of the food, the friendliness of the employees, and the cleanliness of the restaurant. In a bank branch, you may also want to include speed of service and friendliness for the tellers, but you might also add accuracy and security to your list. Construction companies must meet design specs and building codes, while family doctors must comply with regulations on patient privacy and prescriptions. When in doubt about whether an item should be on your list, let your Customer Insight system tell you what is truly critical to your customers and what isn't.

If you have not defined exactly what it looks like to operate with excellence, then you could be having trouble because this makes your people have to guess, and they're guessing wrong. Listen, leaders: when we make our people guess and they get it wrong, that's not their fault. That's our fault.

You can hope they figure it out through trial and error, you can reprimand them until they guess correctly, or you can define excellence with a clear behavioral list.

LEVER 4:
MEASURE IT

What gets measured gets done. If you want to be more consistent on the fundamentals, then another way to increase the excellence is to regularly measure how you're doing. This practice taps into a fundamental drive in humans—we want to win, so we keep score.

There are multiple benefits to measuring things. First, it forces you to be clear. I have been in a lot of strategy meetings with executive teams that believed they were all aligned on what mattered most—right up until they tried to put a number on the scorecard. Measuring performance requires you to agree on how to measure it *and* on what number is good enough to be called a success. I could say I want to get in shape, but that could mean losing weight, increasing my max bench press, or getting my VO_2 max up. And even after I decide to focus on losing weight, there's a huge difference between setting a goal of losing one pound by the end of the year and losing thirty pounds. When you put numbers down on paper, it becomes real.

And measures are not just good for forcing clarity. In fact, one of the most powerful methods for ensuring you don't quit on a new habit is frequent measurement. Each measurement moment serves as a reminder of what we are trying to do and can help us recommit to the standard. Most of the important things in our lives are made up not of single actions but of a series of actions strung together. This is true of relationships, health, and customer experience. The key to success is setting up systems that keep your motivation and clarity high over long stretches of time. If you do want to lose weight, multiple studies have shown that one of the keys to keeping weight off is the practice of weighing yourself daily. It's not always fun (especially the day after binging on dessert), but it does keep your goal at the front of your mind and therefore keeps your motivation high.

For your organization, this could mean moving from a standard of "responsive service" to "we return all client emails/phone calls within twenty-four hours," or going from being okay with "satisfied customers" to "we will earn a 9 or 10 on Net Promoter Score from at least 80 percent of customers within two weeks of serving them."

In some cases, measuring requires you to create a new method for collecting the numbers. When this is necessary, aim for the simplest measurement possible. I've seen many leaders stall here because they attempt to do the most precise and nuanced measurement possible. My advice is to prioritize the speed of measurement instead. For example, I would prioritize stepping on a scale every morning over waiting for the full-body composition scan that you have time to do a few times a year. The goal is to get feedback as close to real time as possible. Lower-quality information that comes quickly is better than high-quality information you get only once in a while. This usually means designing the lowest-friction methods possible.

One example of this is a restaurant franchise owner I worked with who put a webcam in his drive-through window and pointed it at his staff (not at the customers). He then logged into the live feed at random times throughout the day to measure how they were doing. All he looked for was smiling at the customer. He knew that a great customer experience in a drive-through involved more than just smiling, but those other things were harder to measure. So, he less frequently measured those (such as surveys to ask about food quality). However, he realized that smiling was close enough to good service that it could be a useful measure. He would observe ten customers come through and then post what he saw on their private Facebook page ("Scott smiled ten out of ten times! Great job!").

However, don't just use the first measure that comes to mind. Think carefully about what measures you pick. Measurements are powerful, even when you choose the wrong measure. A tragic example of this is Wells Fargo Bank.

In 2013, rumors started swirling about Wells Fargo Bank employees opening accounts in customers' names without their knowledge or consent. It turned out that thousands of employees opened millions of accounts, in some cases ruining the credit score of customers and in all cases violating the law.

Why did this happen? In an effort to encourage growth, the executives at the bank headquarters decided to measure how many new accounts were opened each day in each branch. Branch managers were assigned quotas for the number and types of accounts created. If they did not hit their targets, that gap was added to the next day's goals, pushing them to open even more. And while measurement alone can be powerful, they tied their pay to whether they met these measures, with personal bankers receiving as much as 20 percent of their salary from hitting this goal. The combined pressure from their leaders and their paycheck amount motivated some employees to create unauthorized accounts.

The measure drove a significant behavior change. It was very effective. They opened a lot of new accounts during this program. It just wasn't the right measure, and so it didn't drive the right behaviors.

For better *and* for worse, what gets measured gets done.

LEVER 5:
SHARE THE SCORE

You may have evaluated how you measure and patted yourself on the back. You might have already defined excellence clearly. You might even have a scorecard that you look at monthly. But you might have the score and fail to share the score. The point of measuring is not only that you, the leader, know the score; it's that *everyone* in your organization will know the score.

It's like a basketball coach who makes their team play in a gym with the scoreboards taken off the wall. In this scenario, the coach doesn't mind, though, because they have the game score coming in real time to an app on their phone. They tell their players, "Keep going. I'll tell you when the game ends and if you won or lost." In this situation, the scorekeeping isn't helping the people who are making it happen.

Sharing performance metrics has been proven to be powerful in a wide variety of industries over many years. Charles Schwab (who went on to found a large financial management firm) made his first million as an executive in Andrew Carnegie's steel company. One day, Schwab came by the steel mill with a piece of chalk in his hand. While one shift was going out and the other was coming in, he drew a large number six on the plant's floor. Employees asked what it meant, and he replied, "Oh, that's the number of steel beams the last shift made. I just thought you would like to know."

He then put the chalk down and walked away. When he returned to the plant at the next shift change, what would you guess was written on the floor? It was a number seven. He came back at each shift change to write the "score" on the floor, and within two days, the production in the plant went to ten beams per shift. This 66 percent improvement didn't come from a new training program, new equipment, or even new pay bonuses. It was driven entirely by the power of sharing the score.

During my time at the Chick-fil-A Support Center, we wanted to see if this was applicable with a typical restaurant company. One day, a good friend and colleague of mine invited a group of restaurant employees in the Atlanta area for a special experience as a reward for doing great work. They were told they would be paid to bowl. They arrived, excited and eager to play. They picked out a ball and put on bowling shoes. However, when they got to the lanes reserved for them, they discovered that the screens had paper taped over them, and a bedsheet was hung on plastic pipe frame in front of the pins. They were being told to bowl without a way to keep score.

Each of them started with plenty of energy, picking up the ball and pushing it down the lane. But within an hour they had lost most of their interest. In fact, one brave soul asked how long they had to keep going. My colleague replied that they didn't have to stay at all; it was a bonus experience. The brave employee replied that he had somewhere else he needed to be and started taking off his bowling shoes. Everyone else seemed relieved and agreed that they wanted to go too.

My friend then took the paper off the screens and walked down the lane to pick up the bedsheet blocking the view of the pins. And when he got back, the same bold participant decided to throw one more ball. When he wasn't stopped, the others got excited. And before long, everyone was putting their shoes back on and diving right back in. In fact, they stayed and played for over an hour longer.

Without a score, bowling had become manual labor. It felt like drudgery, they later reported, hefting the ball and shoving it down the chute. You literally couldn't pay them to keep doing it. But when you show a score on a screen, people are not only glad to do it but will pay you to do the exact same activity.

A great business example of this is Springfield Remanu–facturing. They have so fully embraced the power of score-keeping that it permeates the company's entire culture. Everyone is educated on how their role is measured and how that number feeds into the overall score. They have a regular meeting to share the results from the other departments, and it's a high-energy, anticipated meeting. Yes, that's right, it's a numbers-reporting meeting with high energy! Their CEO, Jack Stack (now retired), wrote a book about the story and systems called *The Great Game of Business.* Some of the leaders of Chick-fil-A visited them to see if what they talked about in the book was realistic and found it to be even more impressive in person than it was described in the book. Check it out yourself. It's a great book and an even better company. This really works.

How often should you share the score? Probably more than you are now. If you have the right measure, the more you share it, the better. In my experience, most leaders, including me, don't communicate the important things enough. Studies have shown that it takes a leader saying something seven times before their people remember it and believe that it's important. To be clear, seven times isn't enough to get them to do it right every time; it's just enough to get them to realize that you truly *want* them to do it. It will take saying things a lot more than seven times to make them an integral part of your culture. Post it on signs. Say it in your annual speech every single year; no matter what else you say, be sure to include the critical measures. Bring it up every time you visit a jobsite. Put it in your email signature. Send a monthly video recorded from your phone with you talking about it. Have someone write a song about it.

If you want Operational Excellence, you must communicate the core things as much as possible. Do the maximum, not the minimum.

When your people roll their eyes and finish the sentence for you, then you know you are saying it enough. I don't say that as a dramatic hyperbole. I mean it literally. It should be a joke among your people that you always say the same things about your Operational Excellence standards. They will be smiling at your predictability. And you will be smiling because they will have finally gotten the message.

LEVER 6:
NARROW YOUR FOCUS

I hate including this lever in the list. I hope this one doesn't apply to you. It's not fun, and it's not easy. But time and again, this has turned out to be a necessary step on the path to excellence.

Sometimes, the best move is to do less. If you have nineteen product lines, maybe you should cut them down to nine or ten, or even three to four. You may need to pull out of a region, close an entire division, or even fire some customers.

The more complex your operations are, the harder it is to deliver Operational Excellence. If you have a variety of services and they're all performing around a C+ or B-, then you might need to consider pulling back on some of your offerings and getting your most critical product lines up to A-level excellence. And when that is going smoothly, then you can restart those other projects.

Again, I really don't like this one, but I have had to do it myself. Years ago, I launched a new division in my company. We added a recruiting agency to our consulting company. After two years of hard work, we achieved profitability. Six months later, we shut it down. It was taking 80 percent of our time and delivering 20 percent of our income—and worst of all, we were starting to see the Operational Excellence of the core services slipping because of the demands that this new division put on the core team.

I could have made money by keeping it open, but I would have risked delivering inconsistent excellence on the work that was responsible for 80 percent of our results. That's not a good trade.

I bet you've seen this principle in your life too. It's all over the restaurant space in the United States. I've praised Chick-fil-A for its Operational Excellence, and I think they deserve it. They work very hard to improve this every year, using all the levers I've discussed so far and more. But they're not the only fast-food restaurant chain known for high Operational Excellence.

In-N-Out is also loved by its customers, partly for being consistently excellent. Five Guys has a strong reputation for reliable quality. Raising Cane's is also respected for their hot, fresh food you can count on.

However, if you know these restaurants, you might have noticed a similar theme regarding their menu. They all have a very small menu, four to five items (a sandwich, french fries, drinks, and maybe a milkshake). The less complex the operation, the easier it is to deliver Operational Excellence. When your time, team, and/or money are limited, you can speed up your path to excellence by reducing the number of things you spend them on. You can narrow your focus to improve your excellence.

Once you regain your reputation, then it's much, much easier to expand what you offer. When people trust you, they are much more likely to believe you could do something else with excellence. This is such a well-known phenomenon that psychologists have named it the *Halo Effect*.

If we believe that you are good at one thing, then we see you with a "halo" on your head (like a cartoon angel)—we think everything you do is good. This is why Olympic gold medal winners are invited to speak at business conferences. They may have spent eight hours a day in a swimming pool and may have never run so much as a lemonade stand, let alone a major company, but they *did* win a gold medal. So, we think what they say about other topics must be gold level too.

Knowing this is a built-in human bias helps you plan your customer-trust-building campaign. First, win in a single area. Become known for reliable quality. Then, leverage your Halo Effect to launch your next product with all the good feelings from the first product giving it a boost.

A famous example of this is Amazon. They didn't start as "the everything store." Jeff Bezos had that vision from the beginning, but he very deliberately limited what they sold to books and *only* books for a long time. For many reasons, he believed they could show up strong in the book market. In those early Internet days, online shopping was not trusted. Bezos knew he couldn't afford any failures in Operational Excellence while they were building their brand. Then, one after the other, Amazon added other products until they could legitimately claim they were "the everything store."

Play the long game. Narrow your focus. Build up trust through Operational Excellence, and only then expand your product lines.

LEVER 7:
FIND YOUR BOTTLENECK

Sometimes, I have worked with companies who have been investing in their operational capacity, putting in serious time and effort, but seeing very little return. And after doing an in-depth assessment, we discovered they had a bottleneck in their process. Suppose you are a manufacturing company, for example, and you have eleven steps a product must go through to be fully assembled and ready to ship. In that case, it doesn't matter if ten out of the eleven steps in the process double capacity; if one step remains slow, then the entire line can only move at the speed of that slowest step.

This is widely known in manufacturing companies thanks to the proliferation of the lean manufacturing movement. But the principle applies to other companies, including those in services. The accounting team that splits up the work can present the results only when the slowest member of the team finishes their part. The construction project stops when one key material is delayed getting to the jobsite. And the sales volume during a retail store's busy hours is limited by how fast their cashiers can check people out.

If you've been using the previous principles to make system upgrades and are still not seeing improvements, perhaps you need to find the bottleneck in your system and spend your time improving that area. It doesn't matter how many leaders you put on the other parts of the process or how clearly you measure the entire process if you have a bottleneck that is holding the whole process hostage.

LEVER 8:
OVER-RESOURCE IT

The last lever may or may not apply to you, but it could be a game-changing move if it does apply.

Sometimes, a mature industry gives up on Operational Excellence for one part of its business. It could be family doctors or construction projects we no longer expect to be on time, or even gas station bathrooms being clean. When this happens, you might be able to differentiate yourself from the rest of your industry by figuring out how to deliver excellence at an unprecedented level. How can you do what no one else has figured out how to do? By being deliberately inefficient.

When everyone has given up on an efficient way of getting excellence, sometimes the only option is to over-resource it.

Let's use gas station bathrooms as an example. We have had gas station bathrooms for over one hundred years, and for one hundred years, they've been nasty. Okay, they're not *always* bad, but they are dirty often enough that we don't trust them to be clean and fresh. The floors are sticky, the toilets are dirty, and the walls have scribbles on them. When you're on a road trip and have to make a bathroom break, do you look forward to visiting a gas station bathroom?

You do if that gas station is Buc-ee's, the Texas-based chain I mentioned in a previous chapter. Buc-ee's is slowly spreading through the United States, so you may not have experienced a Buc-ee's bathroom (yet). Imagine a big bathroom with marble (or faux-marble) flooring and high-end toilets in completely private, floor-to-ceiling-walled stalls, all in perfect, spotless condition. Now, imagine a gas station about twice as big as you just did, and you still might not be thinking big enough—the location in Georgia nearest me has 120 gas pumps!

I have asked thousands of leaders in live presentations if anyone has been in a Buc-ee's bathroom and seen a mess, even once. To this day, after years of asking, I still haven't found anyone who has. I certainly haven't. It's a game changer for their business. This is one of the main reasons you stop at a gas station (the other is refilling your car, of course). Because of this consistent cleanliness, they are uniquely trusted in their industry.

How do they achieve this? They over-resource it.

For a hundred years, the standard method was to have Jimmy, the employee who works the cash register, visit the bathroom every thirty minutes to clean it (and sign the sheet saying he did so). This works pretty well, and it's very efficient.

The problem is that every so often, five minutes after Jimmy is done cleaning the bathroom, someone goes in there and makes a mess. And for twenty-five minutes, the bathroom is nasty (assuming Jimmy is reliably there every thirty minutes). We don't encounter a mess in gas stations every time we need to use the bathroom, but we run into them just often enough for us not to trust the cleanliness of gas station bathrooms, just like we don't trust McDonald's ice cream machines.

What should gas station managers do about this? It's not like they can park someone in the bathroom all day long, right? Well, that's exactly what Buc-ee's does. They pay well above the minimum wage to have a bathroom attendant in the bathroom at all times.

To be fair, part of why this works is that it's a big bathroom. I don't think this would work in a single-toilet bathroom. (Can you imagine Jimmy standing in the corner with his back turned? "Don't mind me!") But even with a large bathroom, the Buc-ee's Jimmy doesn't have enough work to do to keep him busy cleaning messes his whole shift. There's a lot of wasted time in this role.

And it's even more pronounced in the men's bathroom. I don't know how it is in other cultures, but we have some unspoken but widely understood etiquette rules for men's bathrooms in America. My wife tells me it's social hour in the women's bathroom. Talking while peeing is no big deal. I've heard that you can make new friends in there!

That's not how it works for men. Even when I walk into the bathroom with close friends, our conversation dies as we cross the threshold. This is not chitchat time. In fact, we don't even make eye contact with each other while we are in there. No one says it aloud, but the message is clear, "Eyes forward, soldier. Keep your eyes on your own business."

We don't even want people to stand in the urinal next to us. Unless there's a long line of people waiting to go, like at a sports stadium, American men know to stand at every other urinal.

Maybe the Buc-ee's women's bathroom attendant is having a great time talking it up with the customers, but Jimmy spends his shift in the men's bathroom cleaning occasionally, talking to no one, and avoiding all eye contact! It is massively inefficient, but it guarantees Operational Excellence in a part of their business that sets them apart in their industry.

To be clear, Buc-ee's does many other things that help them stand out from their peers, including selling high-end fudge and home decor and having a huge "wall of jerky," but their reputation is built on the foundation of being one of the only trustworthy options in an old industry.

If you're in a similar situation, maybe, just maybe, you should consider being exceptionally inefficient so you can be exceptionally excellent.

To ensure you don't think this is just about labor in retail stores, let me share a little about how Nucor Steel became the largest steel company in America. Like Buc-ee's, the Nucor formula for success has multiple factors, from exceptional people (I can personally attest that the top levels of their leadership really care and really know their stuff) to a strong sales approach. But a part of that equation is their investment in their steel mills. One of the best examples is their use of plasma arc furnaces. Nucor started making steel with the first commercial-scale furnace of this type in the United States and changed steel production in the country. Everyone was using blast furnaces when they made this investment. Today, approximately 70 percent of the steel made in the United States is produced using electric-arc furnaces (and the largest portion of that is made by Nucor).

You might think they did this because it produces better steel. It doesn't. Steel is a regulated product. It has to be made to the same standards applied to everyone else. So why would they invest in an expensive type of furnace? (It's a serious investment. In 2022, they invested $100 million, adding a melt shop with a plasma arc furnace in an Arizona plant. This was one of several upgrades with plasma arc furnaces made that year as a part of a multiyear upgrade plan.[5])

While the steel is the same, a plasma arc furnace creates other benefits for Nucor. First, it's faster—a *lot* faster. It takes thirty days for a blast furnace to go from cold to hot enough to make quality steel. (It must reach 1,100 degrees Celsius!) A plasma arc furnace can go from off to ready in only twenty-four hours. Second, it's cleaner. "Nucor's use of recycled scrap-based electric arc furnace technology at all of its 24 U.S. mills enables us to operate at 70 percent below the current greenhouse gas intensity for the steel industry," the company says.[6] It also recycles 90 percent of the dust from its electric-arc furnaces.

There are other benefits, but I think you get the point. They don't need a plasma arc furnace to make quality steel, and they could save a lot of money with standard equipment. But Nucor's cutting-edge technology gives them a valuable advantage over their competitors, many of whom have a thirty-day backlog of work to be done, so they never have to risk having their slow furnace sitting idle. Also, the Nucor sales team makes a big deal out of Nucor being the green choice. All of this has helped them reach 60 percent of the market for mini-mills and scrap metal. That means Nucor produces more steel than the rest of the market combined!

FINAL CHALLENGE

Before I move on to the next gear in the engine, I want to give you one last challenge. We are about to dive into the fancy, fun parts of the engine. We're going to look at the latest in artificial intelligence and talk about throwing red-carpet parties. Creating raving fans can be really fun at times. But as you add those components to your engine, don't forget Operational Excellence. Or, as the best-selling author and speaker Jim Collins says, "Never stop pushing on the flywheel." In his book *Good to Great* (which I highly recommend), he used the analogy of a flywheel. Before combustion engines, the "engine" that would run a mill or factory was often a large stone wheel called a flywheel. They sometimes weighed hundreds of pounds. One person pushing on it could barely move it. But if you got enough people pushing for long enough, it would start moving. It might take all you had to get one full rotation. But if you kept pushing while it was in motion, you could get a second rotation much faster. And then a third and fourth time, it would spin around, faster and faster. As the momentum built, it took less and less to keep it going. And once you got it moving, you could connect smaller gears to it so they could run off the momentum generated by the flywheel. The visible results were attributed to the small gears moving mill parts, but the energy to do work came from the flywheel.

Jim Collins uses this analogy to say that the flywheel is all the fundamentals of your business—and he challenged us that great businesses never stop pushing on the flywheel. No matter how many other creative projects they take on, they don't get distracted from the core operational processes. Because if we lose the flywheel, we lose the trust needed to do all the other things we want to do. As I said when I started this chapter, if you don't get this right, nothing else matters.

I've spent more than twenty years inside great organizations, watching them closely, and they all have a passion for mastering the fundamentals. None of them think they are beyond the basics, often working with a passion for little details that their competitors roll their eyes at. I used to be impressed only by innovations in technology or business models, but while I still think those are cool, these days, I'm even more impressed by a company that nails Operational Excellence every time.

John Wooden might have been the greatest college basketball coach of all time. He led his team to ten national championships in twelve years, and dozens of the greatest pro players of his era came out of his program. Many people can win a championship once in a while, but doing it year after year makes his achievement something worth studying.

When you study Wooden, you see a man devoted to getting the details right. For example, he started the first practice of every season by teachings players to put on their socks; then, he moved on to how to tie their shoes. Seriously. He knew that if they got blisters, it didn't matter how good his practice plan was or how positive their attitude was; they wouldn't be able to get the most out of practice.

To be fair, this was in the 1970s when athletic socks had huge seams on the toes, and if you didn't pull them over the toes just right, they could rub your feet raw. But even with that disclaimer, it was still a shockingly simple thing for a great coach to pay attention to. And that's what made him and his players so consistently great. John Wooden explained it like this: "It's the little details that are vital. Little things make big things happen."[7]

The president of Chick-fil-A, Tim Tassopoulos, gives a presentation to all new staff and new franchisees titled "Success vs. Excellence." Success, he teaches, is our performance compared to others. But excellence is my performance compared to my potential. He goes on to say that we don't measure ourselves against how other restaurants are doing. It doesn't matter if we are better or worse than them. Our standard is our own potential. And we have not yet achieved our full potential. We keep working on the fundamentals of our business because we are pursuing excellence, not success.

And there's one more way the flywheel is a good analogy: if you have stalled, it's hard to get it moving. Going from inconsistent to consistent is a lot of work. This is not a side project you put a team of specialists on for three to six months. It could be that you need to delay other initiatives and pause your big marketing spend until you become consistent with your core. In fact, after working with many companies in many industries, I have yet to see a company with more than ten staff members make major, lasting upgrades in Operational Excellence in less than a year's time. (Very small companies can be much nimbler, but even a small amount of staff slows this process down a lot.)

I wish I had better news, but it doesn't serve you well for me to give you false expectations. If you're going to go on a journey, I want you to know how much food and water to pack. You don't want to estimate wrong and end up halfway to your goal without the resources or energy to keep going.

Operational Excellence is the big beast of the Customer Experience Engine. It's the hardest element to get right, but it's also the most important. It's your flywheel. No matter how innovative you become, never stop pushing your flywheel.

QUESTIONS TO CONSIDER

✿ *What character qualities are you looking for in your staff? How does your interview process help you evaluate that?*

✿ *What chemistry qualities are you looking for in your staff? How does your interview process help you evaluate that?*

✿ *Which competencies do your staff have to bring with them and which of them can you train them on?*

✿ *What are the critical few things that you must get right every time? Do you and your entire leadership team agree on that list?*

✿ *How do you measure your core operational deliverables?*

✿ *How often do you discuss your Operational Excellence measures with your leadership team?*

✿ *How often do you discuss your Operational Excellence measures with all your staff?*

✿ *If you have measures to look at, how big is the gap between your best and worst days?*

✿ *What new role (or special project) could you create to put a leader over a critical area of your engine?*

✿ *Who in your company might be ready for a "stretch assignment"?*

✿ *What projects could be distracting you from building a system of Operational Excellence? How could you stop, reduce, or delay those projects?*

✿ *What has the rest of your industry given up on in getting consistent? How could you over-resource that area and stand out?*

CHAPTER SEVEN

PERSONALIZED SERVICE

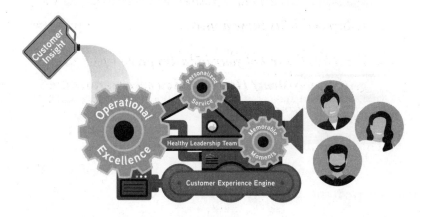

*A*fter we show up with consistent Operational Excellence and learn customers' trust, we have the opportunity to provide Personalized Service.

You probably remember that I talked about the four behaviors of friendly service in the previous chapter, and you might be asking yourself what the difference is between Personalized

Service and the service part of Operational Excellence. Am I going to talk about service skills twice? Not really.

It is true that what most people mean when they say *customer service* I would put in the Operational Excellence bucket. We are going to treat everybody with dignity and respect. *Yes.* And if something goes wrong, we will fix it. *Of course!* If we don't do these well, our customers won't trust us.

If service like that is a part of Operational Excellence, what is Personalized Service?

Personalized Service is moving from reactive to proactive, from standard to custom, from a *professional interaction* to a *personal relationship*.

See, after you have earned their trust, your customers are asking, "Do you care about me?"

This is a fundamental element of our human psychology. We are all asking this question all the time, especially of the people we respect. If they like you (and they will like you if you are delivering Operational Excellence), then they want you to like them too.

They may not be asking this out loud, but deep down, your customers wonder if they are just another transaction or if you see them, understand them, and care about them.

And this is not just for B2C (business to consumer) companies. Even in the B2B (business to business) world, you interact with humans who decide whether to work with you or not. Whether you're B2B or B2C, we're all P2P (person to person). We are all in the people business.

One of my favorite expressions of this comes from Howard Behar (who I got to know during my work at the Chick-fil-A Support Center). He was the president of Starbucks International (now retired). Howard said that Starbucks told their people they weren't in the coffee business, serving people; they were in the people business, serving coffee. Inspired by him, we started saying at Chick-fil-A that we weren't really in the chicken business; we were in the people business. We just use chicken to serve people.

All of us, deep down, want to know that the people we like also like us. We all want to feel like someone cares.

How do we do that for our customers? This can seem like an overwhelming burden to pick up. I don't know about you, but I care deeply about my family and, even after working really hard to show it, I can still fall short.

As noble as this deep love is, that's not what I'm talking about. What I'm talking about is a different kind of relationship, a type that might be new for you. Most of us have a natural instinct to form two kinds of relationships: our inner circle and our outside acquaintances. We devote a large amount of effort and time to the people in our inner circle, and there are very few boundaries with them. We get together often and talk about almost everything that is happening in each other's lives. When we consider the time and energy required to do that for all our customers, we get overwhelmed—well, at least I do. That's why I relegate people in this group to the outside-acquaintance category. I'm glad to see them when we happen to cross paths, but

I will spend no energy to go out of my way to see them, and I share very little of my deepest thoughts and feelings with them.

I'm not challenging the validity of those two relationship categories. I'm introducing a third category: the infrequent friend, the occasional connection, the medium-strength relationship. Human connection doesn't have to be limited to a binary choice between close or distant. There is a wide range of options, a continuum of connections you can choose from. Your customers don't need to be backyard buddies who take up a lot of your time. They just need a few small touches every once in a while to let them know you care.

If you have done your job and delivered Operational Excellence, then providing Personalized Service won't require a lot of time or money. In our diagram of the engine, Operational Excellence is a big gear, more than twice the size of Personalized Service and Memorable Moments. These are little gears in the engine.

Remember the flywheel metaphor, where a large stone wheel needed a lot of effort to get moving? When your family got the flywheel moving fast enough, you could then connect smaller gears that can run off the momentum generated by the flywheel. Your flywheel is Operational Excellence, and the smaller gears are Personalized Service and Memorable Moments.

In my years of consulting, I've seen a lot of companies who have customer service departments that are working way too hard, compensating for inconsistent Operational Excellence. These companies have built up exceptional service skills through making continual apologies and creating last-minute, custom solutions.

They are keeping the customers satisfied through brute force. Unfortunately, every time I have seen this, I have also seen a high-stress and exhausting culture. They operate like an elite team of firefighters, who when woken up in the middle of the night will run across town to put out another customer fire. My team and I now call this *management by cortisol* (cortisol is one of the major stress hormones). This approach works in the short term, but it is not sustainable in the long run.

Instead, when you upgrade your Operational Excellence, you will find that it doesn't take that much effort to make customers feel cared for. Remember, they don't need to feel like your best friend; they just need to know you care about them. Small touches can make a big impact.

I'm about to give you several examples of how other companies are doing this. In fact, I'm going to share more examples than you need—more examples than you should actually *do*. It is not necessary (and can even be counterproductive) to do a lot of personalized touches. Once or twice a year, do one or two things to make a connection and communicate care. If you are showing up with consistent excellence and have earned their trust, then a few small touches will be enough to let them know you care. You can drastically reduce your last-minute crisis-response team and plan for custom communication, delivered when it's convenient for you and without a big budget.

That's enough hype; let's talk about how to put Personalized Service to work.

There are two basic levers you can pull to make this happen: High Touch and High Tech.

HIGH TOUCH

Everyone enjoys being treated like someone special, like they matter to the person they're talking to. Great organizations empower their staff to treat their customers like special guests.

One of the world's best at this is the Ritz-Carlton Hotel chain. Their customers tell story after story of how Ritz goes above the norm to serve them. When you arrive, they greet you by name—before you even check in. If you've been before, they might have your favorite drink waiting for you. One of my friends said he had stayed at a Ritz property for his honeymoon and several years later returned with his wife for an anniversary trip. When he got to his room they had recreated the exact same setup, from roses on the bed to bottles of the same type of champagne. The best part of this example is that they didn't remind the Ritz people of their anniversary.

Part of my job at Chick-fil-A was to study the best brands in the world, and we did a lot of partnership projects with Ritz-Carlton. We talked to their operations leaders, their training teams, and their marketing staff. And we didn't just discuss this in the abstract. We stayed in various locations, dining in steakhouses in their urban skyscrapers and relaxing in their lakeside properties. I know. It was a sacrifice, but someone had to do it.

The feeling they create, the atmosphere people are willing to pay a lot of money to experience time and time again, can't be boiled down to a single thing. It's the combination of several small things, all pointing in the same direction. While you are there, you feel noticed and respected.

Before you limit High Touch to high-cost services, consider In-N-Out Burger. This burger chain, mostly in the western part of the United States as of this writing, has a huge fan base of raving fans. They are a great example of what happens when you deliver Operational Excellence. They also do a great job personalizing the experience for their guests. For example, they have a deceptively simple menu. If you don't know any better, there are only three items you can order: a hamburger, fries, and shakes. (If you include the self-serve soft drink fountain, then there are four items on the menu.) But what their raving fans know is that there are "secret" menu options, allowing you to personalize your order, with fun names like *Animal Style* and *Triple Triple*. You can even have them make you a grilled cheese sandwich, even though it's not on the menu (it's a cheeseburger without the meat). They also use your name when they serve the food and build relationships with their regular customers.

In-N-Out is fast food, on the lowest end of the restaurant spectrum. But they have built a base of raving fans through Operational Excellence and Personalized Service. Don't let your pricing position be an excuse to settle for impersonal service.

With that in mind, let me share some of my favorite High Touch techniques.

ELEVATED LANGUAGE

The lowest-cost option (it's free) is to use *elevated language*. The way you say something changes how it feels. Is it an *estate tax* or a *death tax*? Is it a *rebellion* or a *revolution*? The words you use make a big difference in how people respond. You can say something the standard way and get a standard response, or you can use crass language to rile people up. And you can use elevated language to make them feel special. To be clear, I don't necessarily mean everyone should use formal language. That might be appropriate for your business if you want to create an elegant atmosphere, but the goal is not to sound fancy; it's to sound *unique*. If you want people to feel differently about you than they feel about your competitors, change how you talk to them.

For example, one great way to elevate your language is to *say your customer's name*. Don't use it in every single sentence (that's just weird), but find a way to use their name when you first greet them or when you follow up with them. If you do want to make me feel important, you could call me "Sir." But calling me "Scott" feels even better than calling me "Sir." Learn your customer's name and use it regularly.

Don't just tell your people to do this. Make a system to enable them to do this every time. Remember, the point of this book is not to get you excited or to try to make you care more. I want to help you build a better engine. Don't just hope this happens; bake it into your operations. For example, Ritz-Carlton asks all their staff to greet their guests by name, from their servers in the restaurants to the cleaners pushing a cart down the hallway. In order to help them do that, they have a daily huddle with each shift that includes discussing the guests on the hall, including showing photos of their faces so they can recognize them. And Chick-fil-A has designed their ordering system so that the person working the register can't close out the order without entering a name. Their restaurant staff aren't just disciplined to use names and they don't just care more than other restaurants. They are *forced* to ask, "Can I get a name for this order?" And when the receipt prints out, the name is printed on the top and the team member who delivers the food to the table will read it and verify they're at the right table by using their name.

In addition to using your customers' names, you can *honor your employees* with special lingo. Disney's Theme Parks don't call their employees *janitors* or *retail staff* or *ride operators*. The staff in those parks are called *cast members*. It's a small thing, but it nudges them—and their customers—to see their role as putting on a show to delight the customers.

To switch to a much less glamorous world, I worked with a nursing home chain that replaced the typical name for their patients with "family members," and instead of calling their entry-level staff CNAs (short for certified nursing assistants), they called them *caregivers*. They did the same hard work as other nursing homes, but they truly viewed themselves as caregivers serving family members.

It's not all limited to formal language. You might elevate the experience with humor. Some brands serve their people best by *injecting fun into their communication*. Instead of being fancy, you might want to be funny. One of my favorite personal examples of this is what I have seen at ski resorts all over the world. Each of the trails on the mountain has a creative name. When I was skiing at one of my favorite resorts, Grand Targhee in Wyoming, I saw a sign on the side of the path revealing a run named "The Good." I thought that was a strange name until I saw the next sign, a little farther down the run. This one was titled "The Bad." And then I knew what was coming next. Sure enough, one final sign was around the corner for a run with the highest difficulty. It was called "The Ugly."

That's just fun, and this isn't limited to ski resorts. I've seen restaurants with creative names for their menu items, software with a clever turn of phrase, and even board games with jokes written into the rule books. Southwest Airlines has made safety announcements into my favorite part of the flight. Their flight attendants cover all the necessary information and are hilarious while doing it.

Another example of elevated language is to *ask personal story questions*. At Lowe's Home Improvement stores, their employees are taught *not* to ask, "How can I help you?" or "Can I help you?" It's too generic and the answer customers usually give is, "No thanks. I'm just looking." Instead, Lowe's trains their people to ask, "What project are you working on?" This personalized question sparks a real conversation and a much better customer experience.

Here are some other personalized questions drawn from a range of industries:

- Are you looking for *product one* or *product two* today?
- Who are you buying this for?
- Will you be using this at home or in your car?
- What are you celebrating tonight?

Every person you interact with, whether it's a grandfather on a shopping trip or a corporate executive on a conference call, is a person with a life story. If you want to connect with them beyond the transaction, ask a question that goes beyond the transaction.

For a cool video about this, search "Every Life Has a Story" on YouTube and look for the Chick-fil-A video that should come up in your feed. It was originally a training video from my time as a staff member at Chick-fil-A. For years, we only used it to train Chick-fil-A Team Members, but it's been shared publicly now, so feel free to use it. It's a pretty powerful two minutes, revealing that the people we serve could be going through very different seasons in their life. The ending of that video has this sentence: "Every life has a story, if we bother to read it."

Bonus idea: You could make your own version of this video for your customers. This could be a great tool for teaching your own people to personalize their interactions. Simply stage a typical jobsite with people who look like the range of customers you have, and then walk a camera around the site. Then, drop some words over their heads with compelling stories and put some instrumental music in the background. It's really easy and relatively cheap, as far as training videos go. The hardest part is getting your "customers" not to look into the camera as it moves around the space (it ruins the emotional effect if they do).

Lastly, you can *elevate your everyday language*. Chick-fil-A is widely known for replying to anyone who says, "Thank you" with, "My pleasure." Truett Cathy, the founder of Chick-fil-A, totally stole that from Ritz! It's true. Late in his life, he stayed at the Ritz and was impressed at how they replied to him with, "My pleasure." He said to himself, "That feels nice—and that's free! We can totally do that!" He then came back to Chick-fil-A and urged the staff to make this our response, not relenting until it became a habit across the company. That phrase is so ingrained in their culture that the children of people who work at Chick-fil-A reply the same way, because it's the response they were raised hearing.

Language matters. Of course, it can't transform a bad experience into a good one—we still have to show up with Operational Excellence—but the words we use affect how people feel. Use your words wisely and make your customers feel like you care about them.

SURPRISE GIFTS

One of the most fun ways to make customers feel cared about is to give surprise gifts. The exact gift you give might depend on the type of business you have. A car dealership should probably give things that enhance the driving experience, while a construction company should consider gifts customers can use when they move into their property. To help you identify what gifts you could give, let me share some classic types.

First, you can send your customers a *seasonal treat*. A classic example of this is the Christmas basket with snacks that B2B companies often send to their clients. But listen, if you're sending Christmas baskets to your clients, stop it. Seriously. You're not getting any real benefit from that basket.

I'm not against Christmas or snack baskets. And, yes, they like getting your basket—but you are one of seventeen baskets in the break room. It does not feel special.

What I'd recommend instead is to send a gift basket on another holiday, one that no one else is sending gifts for. I love a good Thanksgiving basket, for example. And you can change it up each year, to keep them guessing. One year it could be summer sausages for Memorial Day, and the next it could be a six-pack for St. Patrick's Day.

Whatever you send, make sure it's a surprise. Expected gifts have minimal impact. When I give flowers to my wife on our wedding anniversary, I don't earn a lot of points from her. That's expected. But when I give her a random rose four months later, she shows it to her friends and talks about it for days.

You don't have to spend a lot of money. It just needs to feel like it's personalized for them—and one of the easiest ways to make it feel personal is to send something customized for *that* holiday or season.

Also, don't just send them your swag (stuff with your logo on it). Swag is cool and customers like it, but it doesn't have the same impact as something that's *for* them and not *about* you. They're not dumb. They know your swag is another way for you to do marketing. They probably send out swag themselves! So, sure, you can make some swag and include it in your gift package if you want, but don't *only* send swag. It feels much less personal.

The second type of surprise gift combines the power of elevated language and surprise gifts by sending your customers a *personalized present*. Instead of putting your name on the gift, put your customer's name on it. For these gifts, the more personal, the better. If you have a client who is passionate about golf, send cutting-edge golf balls with their name on it.

If they love snorkeling, send them an underwater camera with their name engraved on the side. Even better, don't give them a gift with their name on it. Give them a gift that has the name of people they care about on it, such as their spouse. (You know what they're going to do with that gift, right? "Honey, look what I have for you!") If you can make them look good in front of the people they care about, they will love you even more for it.

You might be getting worried about the cost at this point in the conversation. I did say that this is a small gear and that this doesn't have to cost a lot of money. So, how does that work with surprise gifts? How is this inexpensive?

First, remember that I said that you shouldn't do *all* the things I am recommending. It would be too much—and it isn't all appropriate for your business. In my experience, surprise gifts are much more often used by people with fewer clients that pay large amounts. Premium gifts might not work very well in retail (you can't give away a personalized item every time someone buys something), and I don't recommend this if you sell software for consumers (part of the power of your business model is that you can scale without physical constraints). But if you do commercial construction and clients sign $20 million contracts, then a $500 gift is a good investment in the relationship. Or, if you're a financial adviser helping people invest their money and plan for retirement, then keeping a high-net-worth family with you after their matriarch passes away is a big deal, and it's worth spending some money to make them feel cared for.

Second, the gift doesn't have to be huge and epic. Even a little gift they didn't expect can go a long way. Apple puts a sticker in all their product boxes. It's not the world's best surprise gift (for one, it's their logo, so it's not about me), but it's cheap, and it's still nice to get.

As you calculate the cost, consider that gift giving can take the place of some of your more traditional advertising costs. You're reinforcing their loyalty and are arming your raving fans with tools to tell others to buy from you.

Be strategic and compare the cost of the gift with the potential return on investment if they sign up for another year or bring another customer with them next time. Don't spend $1,000 on a customer gift if you're looking to land a $100 contract. But spending $10 on a gift that converts into a $100 sale is a purchase I'll make every single day.

Final challenge: To do this well requires restraint in your communication. If you want to exceed their expectations, you can't promise them a gift in the sales process. That's not a surprise gift; that's a marketing tactic (and they know it). At the beginning of this book, I said you need to maximize the post-transaction experience, to design experiences that leave them loving you more afterward than when they started. This is one of the ways you can do that. You can't overdeliver if you don't first underpromise. Keep your bonus items a secret at the beginning of the relationship and surprise them with a gift.

BONUS SERVICES

Instead of sending a physical gift, many of my clients' companies find it to be more valuable and appropriate to their brand to give their customers bonus services. In addition to delivering what they expected, surprise them with a service they didn't expect.

This can be powerful for businesses that don't sell tangible goods. An IT managed services client of ours (they help maintain all the IT equipment for small- to medium-size businesses) decided to offer free training on office software to their clients. They aren't a training company (officially); they just fix the system when it crashes. But it didn't cost them much to add this, and it made a big impression on their customers. (Plus, as a bonus, it also reduces the user errors that caused some of the system crashes!)

This works even if you work with physical products. Three years ago, I took my car to an auto shop for an engine issue, and they noticed I was almost due for an oil change and changed my oil for no extra charge and without me asking for it. I'm still going to the same shop today—driving past at least ten of their competitors each time. The orthodontist who has put braces on three of my kids hires a professional photographer to do free family photo sessions for his patients. He says some clever stuff about helping us show off their new smiles, tying it back to his business brand. It makes us feel awesome and gives us a story to tell. (I'll talk more about that in the next chapter.)

A homebuilding company we worked with surprises their buyers with a free material upgrade in the middle of the construction process. They pay attention at the early stages, when they are picking their materials, and look for an opportunity to say, "I noticed you were interested in the granite countertops, but then decided not the spend the money on it and chose a cheaper option. Well, we want you to have the home of your dreams, so just this once, we have decided to give you a free upgrade to the granite counters." Or maybe they will upgrade their kitchen sink fixtures without charging them extra for it. (If you have multiple options, I recommend upgrading items in the most commonly used areas. For example, it's better to apply your gift to the kitchen sink than to the bathroom sink in the basement because it will be used more, creating more value for them—and it's going to be easier for them to tell others about your generosity.)

Another homebuilding company we worked with mowed the lawn and trimmed the hedges on the property when the job was all done. They aren't a landscaping company and they didn't tell the customers it was a part of the package, so doing this makes a big impression.

You can plan ahead and provide a free service for your customers, one that surprises them but isn't a surprise to your team or your budget. One of the ways people feel loved and cared for is when we do acts of service for them.

PERSONAL NOTES

No matter what else we do, one surprise gift that will never get old is a personal note. From the beginning of writing, humans have loved getting a personal message from someone they like. It doesn't have to be powerful poetry or even very long. The message can be very short and direct, such as, "I just wanted you to know that I was thinking of you, and I hope you're doing well."

To be clear, when you do this, don't add any sales or marketing materials. This can't be a note to tell them about the new product you have launched or to ask if they are ready to talk about the next contract. Those aren't bad messages, and you should send those to your customers to create sales. The most powerful sales technique is simply to ask them for the sale. But when you do that, it changes the nature of the communication. It does not communicate that you care about them personally. So, send the marketing stuff later or through a different channel. The purpose of these notes is to make a human connection, to tell them that you care.

The ideal version is a handwritten note on real paper. The more technological and digital we become, the more valuable the ancient forms become. Physical mail that isn't an advertisement or a bill is rare. You can stand out by going old school and mailing letters to your customers. And seeing your own handwriting creates a feeling of personal connection that the most beautiful pictures on a glossy page cannot match. To be clear, this isn't convenient or efficient. But the effort and inefficiency of it communicate that you care.

However, I have to confess that for a long time my commitment to the ideal meant that I didn't do this enough. I did this a lot when I was first getting started as a speaker and consultant, and I got great responses. But then I had more and more people wanting to work with me. I started hiring other rock-star speakers and consultants to help me reach more people. They enhanced our ability to help our clients, and the companies we worked with got bigger and bigger. The customers we worked with for each project went from a handful to hundreds to thou-sands at large events. And the bigger we got, the less I sent personal notes.

It's hard to carve out the time and write a note. But personal notes might be the most powerful way to show that you care. Rather than give up on sending a note, I eventually realized that, while a handwritten note on the custom cards was the best format, the other formats didn't have zero value.

If you're busy and if you have a lot of customers, it's okay to send them a digital note. One method that is taking off in popu-larity as of the writing of this book is sending a video message to them, ideally one that has their name and details specific to them in the message. There are a lot of apps and tools that make it easy to do this. But even recording a video might require more time than you have available, so don't look down your nose at sending a personal note via email.

A couple of times each year, I take high-level leaders with me on an epic experience, from Caribbean beaches to the Canadian Rockies. In preparation for a recent retreat, I got out cards in my office to send to the leaders who were coming. It was only about twenty people, so it was a practical option. For weeks, the cards sat on my desk, waiting for me to write a couple of sentences on them. Two days before the event, I still hadn't done it, and it was too late. Even if I stopped what I was doing and wrote the cards and put them in the mail, they wouldn't arrive before the retreat.

So, I just pulled out my phone and wrote a text to each leader. Honestly, I wrote a message that I could copy and paste.

Then I added their name to it and pressed send, twenty times in a row.

Would the handwritten cards have been better than those last-minute text messages? Yes. But the text messages I *did* send were more valuable than the cards I *didn't* send.

Don't overthink this. Just send a note to tell them you were thinking of them.

While this is a good thing for *you* to do, I would much rather see this become something *everyone* on your team does. Remember, my recommendation is not that you should care more or try harder. If your default solution is for you to work longer hours to get more done, then you're not building an engine. To build an engine, a true system of Personalized Service, you need to give your people the freedom to make decisions about service without checking in with their leaders. So much of what makes them feel cared about happens in the moment, when they are face-to-face or on the phone with a customer. If your people have to stop and ask permission for each extra touch, you will miss the moment.

Ritz-Carlton does this very well. They have also empowered their people to do extra things for customers without having to get permission from the top. After extensive training, including examples of what they can do and what they shouldn't do, they enable every one of their employees to spend up to $2,000 to solve a customer problem or create a special experience. And if a staff member learns about a problem, they "own" the situation. Even if they are the house cleaner and the problem is with the television, they are the point person responsible for communicating with the guest throughout the entire situation. They are authorized to call IT, buy movie tickets to rescue the evening, or whatever else they think is necessary. Only after it's all done will the manager be told what happened.

Too many companies turn these special moments into something generic because the frontline staff doesn't have the ability to respond in real time. If you want your staff to do extra things for your customers, they may need extra training, extra tools, and exceptional freedom.

HIGH TECH

As powerful as High Touch is, there are at least two major drawbacks with these approaches. First, they don't scale to large numbers very well. Most of the time, these personal touches get harder to make the more people you serve. Second, they require us to remember that we should do them. And when the whirlwind of daily demands kicks up, it's hard to pull out of the pressures of the day and do things that aren't directly involved with solving the problems in our faces.

One of the prime examples of High Tech Personalized Service is Amazon. They have won best customer service in America awards several times, but every time I'm giving a keynote presentation and ask a room for a show of hands, I find that very few people have spoken to an Amazon staff member. How do they create raving fans if they don't deliver any High Touch service?

First, they have set a new bar for Operational Excellence. They not only have earned our trust with the transparency of their product pages and the speed of their shipping but have also made it very easy to track shipping, make payments, and even return a product. Operational Excellence by itself creates a lot of positive feelings for your company. But Amazon doesn't stop there.

They also have created personalized algorithms to make it feel like a message written just for you. Your Amazon Home page doesn't look like mine. Not only are different products recommended but even the menu options at the top are tailored to better fit the individual user. And your name is near the top of the page too.

The customer experience is totally personalized, without a human having to do it. Before I give you examples of how to do this, I want to make sure I don't lose you. Talking about brands like Amazon can feel like discussing Mars exploration robots with a guy who loves Legos. You may think, "It's cool to hear what they're doing, but I can't apply any of their techniques to what I'm doing." That's not actually true anymore. It's getting easier and easier each year to enhance your service touches with technology. Every month, there are more tools available that can help you proactively reach more people in a more personalized way. Only ten years ago, using technology to deliver customized service required a massive investment of money. But what you can do today for minimal cost is far beyond the best options of those early days. And as I will show you, these tech tools are applicable to more than just online retailers. Even if you are a small company or have a product that requires a lot of manual labor, don't skip over these ideas of how to use technology to enhance your service experience. You might be surprised at how much you can benefit from adding High Tech to your service strategy.

CRM SOFTWARE

Let's start with an underrated tech tool: customer relationship management software, commonly called a CRM. These tools allow you to track all the interactions that any of your staff members have with your future and current customers, categorize your customers however you want, and share notes with each other about each customer. There are many different options, some designed for a narrow niche (e.g., Childcare CRM for childcare centers) and some that are used by almost everyone (e.g., Salesforce).

There is a lot of buzz about how valuable they are, so most of the companies I have partnered with as a consultant have a CRM. These systems can enhance your ability to be personalized in major ways—but only if you actually use them. And very few of the companies I have worked with are using their CRM properly.

When it's working, a CRM will remind you to reach out to a person and will even give you personal information about that customer so you can customize your communication. It will tell you the last time someone from your company talked to them, what they talked about, what they bought from you (and sometimes how much they're using what they bought). It will send them birthday text messages for you. It will send a reminder email if they don't open the first one. It can even let you know that they went on a trip to the beach, so you can ask how their summer vacation went when you next contact them.

I don't know another tech tool that is more useful in creating a Personalized Service system than a CRM. And providers have figured out how to use this in a wide variety of industries. I've seen this used with great effect in construction companies, law firms, retail stores, and many other industries.

The problem is that the system doesn't do any of these cool things if you don't train your team to enter in the right data. To make this work, they have to sync their email to the CRM and capture a summary of any phone calls with clients in the system. The only way you know to ask about their beach trip is if your colleague enters what they learned into the CRM. All of this takes extra effort.

The best analogy I have for how a CRM makes a business better is how physical exercise makes your body better. In each case, no single effort makes a meaningful difference, but a pattern of effort can change everything. You can skip any single workout and it won't matter. You can even do a few workouts, but you still won't be in shape. In fact, as someone who got way out of shape and had to get back into shape, the single most helpful thing I heard from a friend was that, for the first three months, exercise was going to be a net negative experience. I was going to feel *worse* afterward. But if I could stick with it long enough, then my body would adjust, and it would actually feel great to exercise. He was right.

The same is true for getting your CRM to be worth the effort. A lot of companies have installed a system, made their team start to use it, and quit because they didn't see any value from it. Or some of their team enters data and some doesn't. They get a little value out of it but not anything like what they were promised.

No single entry in your CRM will make a big difference to how you serve your customers, but a pattern of consistent entry will enable you to do small things that make your customers feel very cared for.

GOOGLE NEWS ALERTS

This one is more slanted toward B2B companies, but it's so easy (and it's free), so I had to include it. If your business has thousands of customers, most of whom don't do newsworthy things (e.g., a restaurant), this might not apply to you. But for some of you, this simple idea could be extremely valuable. If you want your customers to feel like you notice them and care about them, use Google News Alerts to stay informed about them.

As of the writing of this book, this is a free service offered by Google at www.google.com/alerts. You can enter any search phrase (such as your client's name or business name) you want to stay informed about. From then on, whenever that phrase pops up in the news, Google will email you the article.

I don't use this with all my customers, but it has been quite valuable for several of them. Sometimes, a company will hire my consulting firm to help them upgrade their Customer Experience Engine, to partner with them for a few years to go system by system through the engine and establish new habits. When we do a long-term partnership like this, we enter the name of that company into Google News Alerts. There are also industries we have worked with long enough that we have developed special expertise in. For these industries, we have entered keywords to keep in touch with the latest trends in that space. (For our Fortune 500 clients and some of the Silicon Valley start-ups we have worked with, I have had to get weekly summaries of the most relevant news items. They're just in the news too often for me to get an email every time.)

Why do we do this? This sounds like it's a Customer Insight tool (and it is). But I placed this tip in the Personalized Service chapter because what's even more valuable than knowing about my customer is them knowing that I know.

When I see an interesting article about my clients, I copy the URL of that article and paste it into an email. I add a simple note and hit send. For example, earlier this year, I read an article about one of my former customers, Nucor Steel, acquiring a steel plant in Alabama. They mentioned the name Ron Fox, one of my friends and a GM in Nucor, as the leader of the integration. So, I popped open my email and sent a note to Ron, linking to the article, congratulating him, and saying that it looked like a lot of work.

It took twenty seconds, and it got an instant response.

I care about Ron. I want him to feel like I am paying attention to what he's doing, but I obviously can't scroll through the news every day, looking for things he and every other one of my clients are doing to congratulate them on. So, I set up a Google News Alert to do that for me.

Using Google News Alerts may not be for everyone, but I encourage you to give it a try if you have any clients that might make the news occasionally. I've found it to be an extremely simple way to keep in touch with my clients.

EDUTAINMENT

The information we have today would shock people from earlier times. Frankly, the amount of information and options we have today would shock *us* if we could tell our younger selves twenty-five years ago what is available today. It's not slowing down either. Huge portions of the world that have never connected to the Internet are coming online. They will not only consume all these materials but will create more data, more messages, and more options for us to decide on.

It is overwhelming and literally impossible to keep up with what is going on in our own field. I just listened to a podcast this morning that said every year, there are 1.8 million new medical articles published in reputable medical journals. That is more than 4,900 new articles every single day. There may be a breakthrough in treatment for the medical problem you are talking to your doctor about that was published the same morning you are in the doctor's office, but it might be years before your doctor becomes aware of that breakthrough.

Trusted guides are really valuable, and they are only going to increase in importance in the coming years. If you can become someone who helps people cut through all the clutter and make better decisions, that would be a true service to your customers.

But the information can't be dry or take a long time to process. With all the many messages that are flooding all our lives, people won't engage with something that isn't entertaining. But when you combine education and entertainment, you get *edutainment*. It's fun, interesting, and engaging for your customers. Plus, it's timely, insightful, and useful.

More and more companies have begun to provide edutainment, which is sometimes also called *content marketing*. Some send a monthly newsletter, others host a podcast, and some go as far as hosting a YouTube channel or even doing keynote speeches at industry conferences.

If you want this to work, though, you have to do more than build an online library of information and tell your customers to look it up when they need it. To make this feel like Personalized Service, you need to use technology to send helpful information to your customers before they ask for it. Remember, Personalized Service is going from *reactive* to *proactive*.

Amazon is a really interesting case study. As of the writing of this book, they have made a big push into proactive communication—maybe too much so! They started with "similar products" listed below the main product info. Then they added "recommended for you" on the home page. These were widely received as positive. For me, it was the only advertising online I was glad to see.

But then they started pushing even further into proactive messaging, especially with their Alexa devices. If you have ever had the experience of Alexa interrupting your conversation to answer a question you didn't ask her, you know what I'm talking about.

For a purer example of helpful information, consider Netflix. Part of Netflix's great user experience is that they are good at recommending shows I will like.

But this goes far beyond software companies. I subscribe to several companies' newsletters to keep me up-to-date on industries in which we do a lot of work, including construction (Granite Rock), health care (Life Force), and entertainment (Dragonsteel). Others put out podcasts that I listen to weekly, including Seth Godin (marketing guru), Harvard Business School (finance and management), and Gary Keller (founder of Keller Williams, a massive real estate company). They discuss trends in the overall industry, share their personal learning, and add their opinion on what's happening in their category.

One of my client companies is Elephant Learning. They have an online portal where kids can learn a year of math in three months. That's a bold claim, one that they have backed up by doing research then having it validated by outside experts. Yes, they have the usual marketing videos of satisfied customers, but they also have academic white papers outlining the core methodology and learning outcomes. (The founder of that company earned a PhD in mathematics, so he knows a bit more about how to transfer core math concepts to kids than most people). You might be thinking, *How is a white paper "entertaining"?* Sure, for some of his customers, these white papers might seem complicated and unnecessary. However, some of his clients are school administrators, who have master's degrees in education methodology. For them, these are not only useful (assuring them they are bringing in valid tools) but are easy to read and engaging. Just because it's a white paper doesn't mean it has to be boring.

There are many support tools for people looking to do this, from software to plan your content schedule, to conferences to learn how other creators are doing it, to people you can hire to do content creation for you. Just search "content marketing" online to find a ton of information. If those search results are overwhelming and you would like some advice on where to start, I recommend the work of Joe Pulizzi, including his book *Epic Content Marketing*.

All this edutainment can be an effective way to draw in new customers and keep your customers engaged. As one of my mentors, Truett Cathy, often said, "If you help enough other people get what they want, eventually you'll get everything you want." Don't spend your trust by always pushing your customers to buy from you. Use your expertise to help your customers make better decisions, and they will feel like you see them as a person, not just as a sales opportunity.

ARTIFICIAL INTELLIGENCE

I will close out this discussion of High Tech ways to deliver Personalized Service with a cutting-edge trend. If I update this book in ten or twenty years, this section will almost certainly need to be rewritten. That's because I'm going to talk about artificial intelligence, or AI.

Before I talk about how to use AI to make your customers feel cared for, I need to bust a myth. Most of us have learned what AI is by watching movies. In those stories, dabbling in AI causes the robots to revolt and to kill us all. As of the time of this writing, we don't know how to make AI like that (yet). There's a debate on whether we will ever be able to make that kind of intelligence (for better and for worse). I won't get into that here. I only want to point out that once we get past the movie myths, we discover that AI is already here—and it's a powerful customer service tool.

AI is already doing a lot to make our lives better, maybe more than you realize, and we have only seen the beginning. Just a handful of years ago, AI was expensive and required your own team of experts to build a custom tool. Only the biggest companies could afford it, and only those whose business was directly involved in AI were working on it, such as Google or Palantir.

That is rapidly changing. You can now rent AI services, either using their existing solutions or even hiring them to make a custom solution for you. More and more businesses are using this to enhance their service experience, including a lot of companies you might not think would use AI.

It's a lot like how businesses thought about websites twenty-five years ago. They were hard to build and required a specialist to create and maintain, and most people didn't think their business needed a website. Today, if you don't have a website, people naturally wonder if you're a real business.

I'm predicting that by 2030, seven years from the writing of this book, you will be either using AI or you will be struggling.

By then, if not sooner, AI will have spread so far and wide that the question is not *whether* you are using AI in your business but *which* AI system you are using.

What do you actually do with AI? How could AI help you make your customers feel cared for? I will highlight two ways AI tools have been helpful to some of our client companies. The first is finding patterns in big data sets, and the second is custom communication.

AI is not just for software companies. Some of the biggest users of AI are those who manage a lot of physical assets. Thanks to the explosion of small, cheap sensors, we are now building our equipment and tools with sensors embedded. AI can track the performance of these machines and detect a breakdown long before a human would notice. Some of these systems are so good that they can tell you a breakdown is about to happen, warning before it occurs so you're not surprised and unprepared.

These companies are proactively helping their customers by keeping an eye on the equipment and serving them well. One of the companies I spent time with last year sells industrial cranes to ports. They have built a strong fan base and are rising to the top of their field, due in part to their premium level of service and repair. Every day the cranes are down costs ports a lot of money. So, we talked about setting up AI to track the cranes, which would allow them to send a service team to that port *before* the crane goes down.

AI isn't just for big, industrial companies, though. My wife drives a GMC Yukon that came with the OnStar hardware and service. This includes a monthly email from GM with info on our vehicle's performance, like how much time until the next oil change and the tread life on the tires. The more advanced features of OnStar can detect when you have been in a crash, automatically calling for help if it's severe enough. That's all done by AI working in the background and gathering information about her car and driving patterns.

If you manage a lot of equipment or have many moving parts in your business, adding AI might allow you to be proactive and customized with your communication.

The other application of AI I will mention is how it is revolutionizing communication. AI is able to translate from speech to text or vice versa nearly perfectly. AI can even translate between languages in real time—including for live speakers. (I just read about a new AI system that learns the voice pattern of the person speaking and then uses their tone and pitch when translating to make it sound even more like the individual speaker's voice.)

You have probably experienced AI more than you realize. If you have used any chat windows for help online, then you almost certainly were not talking to a real person, but an AI "bot." There are entire newsletters sent by AI (check out Futureloop by Peter Diamandis for my favorite example of this). Google Assistant has created an AI bot that is capable of syncing with your calendar and making a live phone call to schedule appointments for you. Search for "Google Assistant Scheduling Hair Appointment" on YouTube for a two-minute demonstration.[8]

I have shared a portion of this video in my keynote presentations and strategy workshops for a few years, and every time, most of the people in the room are blown away with how lifelike it is. It even includes speaking cues like "uh" and "mm-hmm" to sound more lifelike. Audiences are more shocked when I reveal that this video is from 2018. This kind of AI interaction has been happening for years. It isn't a new, wild experiment that only Google executives can use. You may have been on the phone with an AI bot already and not known it.

If you're overwhelmed at keeping up with a large customer list, or if you have customers calling you at all hours of the night for answers to your most common questions, then AI might be able to make you more proactive and faster, without you having to work long hours.

Again, it's not a requirement that you incorporate AI into your business—not yet. But it's only a matter of time. And I recommend you get ahead of this curve rather than be the last one to use these increasingly affordable tools to make your customers feel cared for.

DON'T TOLERATE YOUR
EXCEPTIONAL EMPLOYEES

Let me give you one more challenge as you think about building your Personalized Service system: Don't tolerate exceptional performers.

You can probably think of someone on your team who your customers love more than the others. Maybe Diego always gets higher ratings after a customer visit or customers get in Kayla's checkout line, even when it's the longest line in the store. Maybe you have even asked if Diego has a brother or joked about cloning Kayla.

Don't tolerate this in your business.

Yes, of course, I hope you have exceptional performers, people who make amazing connections with your customers and do extra things to serve their clients. I'm not saying this is bad. But I want to shake you out of your complacency regarding them. Why are you allowing them to be the only one who creates these kinds of connections? What if you could get all of your service people to be just as personalized?

I'm good with their level of performance. I'm not okay with them being the exception from the norm.

One of our longtime clients is a commercial roofing company. Unlike residential roofers, the real money in the commercial side of the roofing business is in the long-term relationship. They don't just want to build a roof; they want to have the contract to maintain that roof for years to come. When I was teaching this company about Personalized Service, one of their leaders spoke up and said that this sounded a lot like what their best account representative did. Intrigued, I asked for details. He proceeded to tell me about Tim.

Tim did a lot of extra things to make their clients feel cared for. For example, Tim bought a cooler and filled it with drinks for his customers. Not just any drinks, either. He found out their favorite drink and put it in the cooler. When he showed up at a campus to talk to the facilities manager (his main point of contact), he didn't wait for a request. He pulled out the customer's favorite drink, handed it to them, and only then started the conversation.

I thought this was brilliant. Some of you might want to do this for your clients. But that's not my point in sharing this story. See, after I geeked out about how creative that was, I had to ask them, "Why is Tim the only account rep with a cooler of drinks in his service truck?" These are multiyear, million-dollar contracts, and it's a $25 cooler.

Before you hire a consultant and take a two-day retreat to create a Personalized Service system for your company, maybe you should take a look at what your best people are already doing. You might have everything you need to build a Personalized Service system right now. Your exceptional employees might already being doing it. You just need to stop tolerating everyone else not being like them.

When it comes to service, most people seem to assume that it's just one of those things you can't do on purpose: "Some of our employees just are good with people and some aren't. There's nothing we can do about it." Don't believe that myth. Don't settle for hoping your people are nice and care. Make a strategic plan. Put a team together. Give them training. Give them tools. Build a system of Personalized Service.

QUESTIONS TO CONSIDER

✿ *What words or phrases do you frequently use in your business?*

✿ *How can you elevate some of them to make your people stand out or make your experience just a little more special?*

✿ *What gifts could you give to your customers?*

✿ *Can you add something to an existing delivery? Or is there a unique item or experience you can give them?*

✿ *When would your customers not expect to receive a gift?*

✿ *What services could you surprise your customers with for free?*

✿ *What goes along well with what you're already doing?*

✿ *What free upgrades could you give them?*

✿ *Who could you partner with to provide related extra services?*

✿ *What could you teach your customers that would build trust in your company?*

✿ *What medium would be easiest for you to get started? Writing a newsletter? Recording audio for a podcast?*

- *Who on your team would be good at creating edutainment content?*

- *How well do you use your CRM software?*

- *What would it mean to be one step better at integrating that system into your operations?*

- *What equipment or data sets could AI help you track?*

- *What routine communications could AI take over for you?*

- *Who are your best service providers?*

- *What are they doing differently than all your other service staff?*

CHAPTER EIGHT

MEMORABLE MOMENTS

*I*f you have done all the other things I've talked about so far—if you've understood your customers deeply with a system for Customer Insight, earned trust with an Operational Excellence system, and made them feel cared for by building a system that provides Personalized Service—then they love you. But just because they love you doesn't mean they are talking about you.

People don't tell facts; they tell stories. If you want your customers to tell others to buy from you, then you have to create a story-worthy moment—a Memorable Moment they will share with others.

Before I tell you how to make this happen with your customers, I have to point out two common misconceptions.

First, you don't create Memorable Moments through great advertising. I have had the privilege of participating in some of the best advertising in the history of the United States. Several of the companies I have worked with are considered advertising trendsetters, and the advertising campaign of Chick-fil-A has been inducted into the National Advertising Hall of Fame. Those black-and-white cows spelling "Eat Mor Chikin" on a billboard is brilliant, and they have managed to take that idea and run with it to create a wide range of entertaining and clever advertising. (Just to be clear, I did not come up with this campaign and cannot claim responsibility for its success. I just had the chance to work with the marketing department on how to make best use of these assets, so I was entirely on the learning side of the equation in this case.)

If you happen to come up with an advertising campaign like this, then I recommend that you run with it. Advertising is important—but it serves a different function than Memorable Moments. I believe the best use for advertising is to grow your share of mind. That's marketing lingo for how likely it is that when your customer thinks of your category they will think of you. If they're hungry, do you even come up as a restaurant option in their mind, or did they forget you existed?

Funny ads and musical jingles are designed to stick in your customers' minds and increase the odds that they will buy from you.

Increasing mindshare is a good thing to do. But this isn't a book on share of mind or advertising. The purpose of this book is to help you upgrade your customer experience, and the goal of Memorable Moments is to get your existing customers to talk about you. People will talk about a funny advertisement they saw, but that's not as powerful as them telling someone else about why you're so good at what you do and urging them to buy from you. To get that response, you have to do more than advertising.

Second, if you want your customers to talk about you, the story can't be about how awesome you are. This is counterintuitive and *really important.* You might think the best way to get your customers to tell others to buy from you is to emphasize how good you are at what you do. You might be able to convince them that you are that great. But even if they believe you are good at your job, they don't want to tell *your* story; they want to tell *their own* story.

I'm going to use Star Wars to flesh this out. The Jedi robe and lightsaber in my closet might have something to do with why I picked Star Wars, but even if you're not a big fan, I think it will help this idea come to life.

Why do I love Star Wars so much? Largely, it's because I wish I could be a Jedi. I would love to jump twenty feet while doing flips. It would be so cool to move things with the power of my mind. Whether you like the movies or not, I think we all want to feel special. We all want to be Luke or Rey. We want to believe we could be more than just a moisture farmer or scavenger. (Just to be clear, I want to be young Luke, not deadbeat dad, depressed, old Luke. I'm still trying to get over how they ruined that character! He almost dies trying to redeem his dad but he's quick to try to kill his nephew?! Okay, sorry, my nerd rant is over. Back to the business content.)

When we tell stories focused on how great we are, we are hoping that if we convince our customers that we really are a Jedi, they will tell others to come see what we can do. It won't work. They might even believe that you are a Jedi, but if you want them to tell this story to others, you can't be the hero of the story. Your customer needs to be the hero of the story.

They don't want to tell your story; they want to tell *their* story.

So, if we don't play the role of Luke, who do we get to be in the story? We do have to show up or there won't be any business value for us when they share the story.

We play the role of Yoda. We are their guide, a wise mentor who helps them realize they really are a Jedi.

You might notice that this analogy is used by Donald Miller in his excellent book *Storybrand*. That's not a coincidence. I actually went through a similar research journey, sitting under the same gurus and attending the same certification programs. I didn't help him with his work nor he with mine, but we did drink from the same well. And since then, I've applied these ideas with a wide range of industries, from construction to call centers, from SaaS start-ups to steel manufacturers. These aren't just good ideas; they're proven customer-activation methods.

Whatever your industry, you don't inspire them to talk about you by making yourself look like a Jedi; you do so by making *them* feel like a Jedi. See, at this stage of the customer journey, the question your customers are asking is: *How do I feel about myself when I'm with you?*

This question is not something most people explicitly ask. It may be subconscious, but we're all asking this question all the time. This is a big part of how we choose what goes into our lives, from our clothes to our music to our friends.

Do your customers feel like the best version of themselves when they are with you? Do they feel proud of the story they are living in when they are using your products?

All the great brands have found a way to tap into our primal desires. Raving fans of these brands, who wear the T-shirts and slap the stickers on their cars, the people who talk about the products and share their experiences over a dinner with others, these people aren't just talking about brands they love. They are using those brands to prove to themselves and the world that they really are a Jedi.

This all sounds noble and beautiful, but it may not sound like normal business operations. First, let me share some examples of how other brands have done this, and then I will give you a process you can use to figure out your own version.

Harley-Davidson might be a fun place to start. I could have organized this entire book around Harley-Davidson. When your customers tattoo your logo on their body, you might have raving fans!

If you ask Harley-Davidson customers why they love Harley so much, most of them will talk about the specs of their bike. They make a good machine. Remember, Operational Excellence is first in sequence and in priority. (Note: If you follow Harley, you might have noticed a decline in popularity from their heyday. From what I can tell, they lost their Operational Excellence, became inconsistent on the fundamentals, and their reputation suffered. But they are back and offering a remarkable customer experience now.)

Harley customers also talked about the custom choices they made. There's no such thing as a "standard" Harley. Every part can be customized, from the wheels to the engine to the handle-bars, and every hog rider I know has put their personal touch on their bike.

What they might not talk about is how they feel when they're on their bike. My research revealed that they feel wild, free, and a little bit dangerous. The rest of their life might have become domesticated, but their Harley proves they are still a *bad mamba jamba*. Monday through Friday, they might drive their kids to soccer practice in a minivan, but on the weekend, they can hit the open road on their bike and feel like a Jedi.

That's why they proudly put the Harley-Davidson logo on their jacket, their helmet, even on their body. It's a signal of their free and dangerous spirit.

However, before you think that the key to Memorable Moments is a sense of danger, I should point out that Volvo has raving fans too. There are people who only drive Volvos, buy Volvos for their kids, and don't understand why anyone would drive anything else.

Why? First, Volvo has good Operational Excellence in that their machines are consistently dependable. Second, you can personalize your car, selecting from a range of models, extra features, and colors. And you can probably guess what they feel when they are driving the Volvo. My research says they feel safe—and also a little bit smug. ("Why would anyone drive anything other than the safest car on the road?!")

Which feeling is better: dangerous or safe?

What do your customers want to feel? For some businesses, customers want to feel danger and wildness. For others, customers dream of safety and security.

If you don't have a ready answer, you don't have to guess. When you build a good Customer Insight part of your engine, it will reveal what resonates with your customers.

Let me share a few more examples, then I'll offer some ideas on how to figure it out with your customers. Apple is a fun example of this. They began with a small number of deeply devoted customers, and they have grown that to a large number of raving fans, and as of the time of this writing, they're the number one or number two most valuable company in the world (depending on the week). Of course, they have earned high trust through Operational Excellence, and they have made it possible to personalize all their products, from color of the case to the apps on the screen. You can even get your name engraved on some of their products for free.

But what pushes them over the edge, what makes some of their customers put Apple stickers on their cars and line up overnight to get the latest product, is how they make their customers feel about themselves. The Apple ethos says (in my words, not theirs), "I'm more creative and cool than most people. I'm not a jerk about it, but, yeah, I'm one of the special ones."

From their famous 1984 ad to the older, overweight, balding "I'm a PC" guy standing next to the young, cool "I'm a Mac" guy, they have been consistent in their theme, and it's working.

One of my favorite examples of this is what a good friend of mine at the Chick-fil-A Support Center did for years. I won't call him out for it, but he was a marketing executive, and our mutual friends can probably guess who I'm talking about. For many years, the required company laptop was a PC. Chick-fil-A now supports both Mac and PC for their corporate staff, but back then, we couldn't use Apple products on the company system. Every two years, they replaced our laptop with a newer one (not the latest model; just one that was less used). And every two years, my friend slapped an Apple sticker over the PC logo on the top of his laptop!

It didn't make his machine cooler than mine, but it *did* help him communicate to himself and the rest of us that he was still a creative and cool guy, even though he was forced to use a PC.

It's not about how cool the brand is on its own; it's about how cool the brand makes me feel about myself.

For a business-to-business example, we can look at IBM. For many years, IBM presented themselves as the wise, safe choice. "Nobody got fired for hiring Big Blue," the old refrain goes. When business leaders wanted to look like a responsible leader with good judgment, they signed a contract with IBM. Their competitors might have figured out how to manufacture similar products, but they weren't able to manufacture the same feelings in their clients as IBM.

Also, a lot of CEOs in the Fortune 500 have hired the consulting giant McKinsey, paying very high prices specifically so they can demonstrate how serious they are about making a big change. I know this because many of them publicly said this was the reason they hired McKinsey.

There's no single "correct" feeling for all companies to create, because humans are different. Some people dream of being one type of Jedi, and others want to be the opposite. What kind of Jedi do your customers want to be? How do they want to feel about themselves? Remember, if you don't know, you don't have to guess; you can simply go upstream and increase your Customer Insight.

Specifically, the process of figuring this out involves answering two questions:

1. What is unique about you?
2. What do your customers want to feel?

Some companies can talk about being true locals, about how they have been serving their community for generations. But other companies can declare that they are not just a local company but are national (or international), with all the resources and expertise that comes with being bigger. Which feeling is better? It depends on you, and it depends on your customers.

Some companies might want to highlight cutting-edge technology and innovative thinking, while others in the same industry might emphasize their tried-and-true methods and resulting reliability. Which feeling is better? It depends on you, and it depends on your customers.

This process combines art and science. You need to stay within the constraints of your situation and leverage what is truly unique about you. If you're not a national company, you shouldn't claim to be one. But you can create a new feeling, carving out a new niche in your industry. Tesla decided to make electric cars fast and cool—and to make their car *owners* feel fast and cool. Before Tesla, electric cars looked very different than sports cars, and the onboard screens encouraged you to go slower and be more energy efficient. When Walt Disney pitched Disneyland to his top staff, they rejected the idea because at the time theme parks and carnivals were known to be dirty, seedy, raucous experiences. No one thought that theme parks could be a child-friendly playground.

So, while you do need to be honest about your own unique features and get clear on what your customers want, you also have the opportunity to create a whole new niche in your industry. Most of the great brands did.

If you have figured out what you want your customers to feel about themselves when they are with you, then the next step is to figure out what Memorable Moments you can create to give them that feeling, and to give them a story to tell.

One of my favorite examples of Memorable Moments is the Chick-fil-A Daddy-Daughter Date Night. I have three daughters, and we have loved these nights. Each local restaurant decides when (or if) to host these events, and none are advertised anywhere beyond their location's Facebook page and on the bulletin board inside the restaurant. You have to know to look for it—often just before or after Valentine's Day in February.

Each year, I reserve a time on their website, and they're ready for me when I arrive. Outside the restaurant, I have seen a horse-drawn carriage or a limousine. Dads and daughters take turns getting a ride. They go around the restaurant once, and then you get out and give the next dad a turn. It's not a long ride, but it is enough to make my girls light up. Inside, they have live music (the franchisees often ask if any of their staff play an instrument like the harp or cello), and half the tables are reserved for the special event.

Those tables are covered with black tablecloths and the staff come to your table to take your order, just like a fine-dining restaurant. And on the table are cards with discussion prompts, with questions like, "What was your favorite toy growing up?"

It's simple and precious. My girls loved it. They got to dress up in fluffy dresses that twirled really well, then eat a big pile of chicken nuggets. It was everything they loved—and Daddy's attention took it over the top.

What's the cost of this evening? Almost nothing, beyond the time to set up the room. Seriously. The food we order at the table is priced slightly higher than usual, covering the cost of the carriage rental.

What's the impact of this evening? Huge. Little girls grow up associating Chick-fil-A with feeling like Daddy's princess.

And dads feel like they just won Father of the Year. In fact, many of the local stores train their team to tell dads on the way out, "Thanks for being the kind of dad who would bring his daughter to something like this. The world needs more dads like you."

This costs Chick-fil-A very little money. But it creates moments that those little girls and their dads will never forget. One year, to fit this in my calendar, we had to go to a Chick-fil-A location that was not near us (it was doing the Daddy-Daughter Date Night on a different night than the restaurants close to us). To this day, whenever we happen to drive past that restaurant, my girls comment on that being the restaurant we went to for a Daddy-Daughter Date Night. It's been ten years.

And it's not just my girls who talk about it. I certainly posted the pictures of me and my girls that Chick-fil-A oh-so-helpfully sent to me. I may have shared them multiple times on multiple platforms. (The world really needs to understand how good of a dad I am!)

One of my favorite Chick-fil-A Memorable Moments is called the Stuffed Animal Sleepover. For this event, your child is invited to bring their favorite stuffed animal (Mr. Bunny or Koojoo the Monkey) to the restaurant on a Friday evening. They can leave their stuffed friend to have a sleepover with all the other stuffed animals and then come back on Saturday morning to pick them up. Before closing the store on Friday night, the Chick-fil-A staff will take pictures of the stuffed animals in various poses, sitting at a table eating ice cream, playing on the jungle gym, and tucked in blankets, sleeping together. The child arrives to not only pick up their stuffed animal but to receive pictures showing the fun Mr. Bunny had and the silly things Koojoo the Monkey did.

Of course, those pictures are sent to you digitally, so they're easy to share. Oh, and what do you think the child wants to do when they show up for drop-off and pickup? Eat dinner and breakfast. So, not only is the cost minimal (only the staff time to take and send the photos) but they also get a boost in sales from the visits.

Each Chick-fil-A restaurant aims to do an event like this every month. There are moments for mothers and daughters, fathers and sons, 5K runs for charity, toy giveaways for children in the hospital, veteran-appreciation dinners, teacher celebrations, birthday parties for longtime customers, and more. And all the attendees are given pictures—which they share with the world just like I did.

In fact, Chick-fil-A has become the most talked-about brand in America on social media—not the most talked-about restaurant chain; the most talked-about *brand* of any kind. And last time I checked the numbers, it was 86 percent positive. (I don't know if you noticed, but that's not the normal percentage of positive vs. negative comments for social media.)

After reading this, you might be thinking, *That's cool for Chick-fil-A, but I don't think it would work for me. I'm pretty sure no one wants to do romantic dinners on an electrical installation jobsite.*

You're probably right about that. But that doesn't mean you can't create a Memorable Moment around your business. Maybe you can do something like what some of our construction company clients have done. The end of every construction project is a prime opportunity. When we worked with a home-building company, we asked them what they do at this transition point. They assured me that they cleaned up the jobsite with excellence and sent the final customer survey. When I pressed further, asking what they did after it was all done, they got confused. One person finally said, "Um, we invoice them."

After some discussion and brainstorming, they added a new step to the closing of a project: they started rolling out the red carpet, literally.

They bought a handful of red carpets (which were not that expensive) and kept them in the trunk of some company cars. Then they planned a closing party for their homebuyers, which included walking down the red carpet, being handed their keys, and even a housewarming basket of goodies from local businesses. The focus was on their customers, not the builders, celebrating their new beginning.

Another of our commercial construction companies, who is a subcontractor on big projects, does this at the end of the project by taking the entire team to dinner at a nice restaurant (usually a high-end steakhouse) and celebrating the close of a successful project. My favorite part is when they give out awards to the other subs as well as the general contractor—and they're funny. One might award Jim as "Most Likely to Drop His Phone Down the Trash Chute" (because he did) and honor Franco for "Best Singing Voice" (because he was constantly singing on the job).

You don't have to be in construction to celebrate the end of a project. Anytime you have a project coming to a close, you have an opportunity to make your customers feel like Jedi.

But even after this, you may still think this is impractical, especially if you have thousands of customers (maybe millions) and there's no way you can afford to put on a live event for each customer. That's okay. Maybe you can learn from one of the ways Apple does Memorable Moments. Yes, in addition to their award-winning advertising, they have created a lot of Memorable Moments for their customers, from the huge secrecy and hype around their product-launch events to their product packaging.

That's right, I think the cardboard boxes their products come in create a Memorable Moment. Apple thinks so too. They have actually patented their packaging.

What's there to patent in a cardboard box? A lot of little things, from the plastic wrapping (note the special tabs) to the fact that the first thing you see when your box opens is your device perfectly placed on a little pedestal like it's a piece of art. There are multiple layers inside, including cool containers for the cords and even Apple stickers. They want your experience of opening the box to be special.

I have shared this example in hundreds of presentations to live audiences, and I conduct an unscientific test to see if it's working. I ask everyone who still has an Apple product box sitting around their home or office that they haven't thrown away yet to raise a hand. And I'm astounded every time to see 70–80 percent of the room with a hand in the air.

I believe they have created a Memorable Moment via their box-opening experience. It makes people feel like they are creative and cool to have a device this special, and they don't want to lose that feeling, so they hang on to the box.

How could you elevate your box-opening experience?

In the days before we could sign documents via the Internet, closing on a contract was a big moment. People gathered in a conference room and passed a set of papers around. It was very official and a great chance to make your customers feel special. E-signing has eliminated this moment, but some of my clients are recreating it. They're still using e-sign software because it is truly so much more efficient. But after everything has been signed, they print their contract on high-quality paper and put it in a fancy leather folio, with their logo and their customers' logo embossed on it. Then, they hand-deliver the contract to their clients at a time that's convenient, often taking them out to dinner while they are in town. They tell their clients that this is a symbol of how much they value this relationship and how glad they are to be partnering with them. The goal is to create something so good-looking that they will put it on display in their offices.

CD Baby, which in the early days of the Internet (before iTunes) was the largest online store for independent music, made one small change that had a huge impact.

Here is the story in the words of CD Baby founder, Derek Sivers, from his blog:

When I first built CD Baby in 1998, every order resulted in an automated email that let the customer know when the CD was actually shipped. At first this note was just the normal *"Your order has shipped today. Please let us know if it doesn't arrive. Thank you for your business."*

After a few months, that felt really incongruent with my mission to make people smile. I knew I could do better. So I took twenty minutes and wrote this goofy little thing:

Your CD has been gently taken from our CD Baby shelves with sterilized contamination-free gloves and placed onto a satin pillow.

A team of 50 employees inspected your CD and polished it to make sure it was in the best possible condition before mailing.

Our packing specialist from Japan lit a candle and a hush fell over the crowd as he put your CD into the finest gold-lined box that money can buy.

We all had a wonderful celebration afterwards and the whole party marched down the street to the post office where the entire town of Portland waved "Bon Voyage!" to your package, on its way to you, in our private CD Baby jet on this day, Friday, June 6th.

I hope you had a wonderful time shopping at CD Baby. We sure did. Your picture is on our wall as "Customer of the Year." We're all exhausted but can't wait for you to come back to CDBABY.COM!![9]

That one silly email, sent out with every order, has been so loved that if you search the web for "private CD Baby jet," you'll get thousands of results. Each one is somebody who got the email and loved it enough to post it on his website and tell all his friends.

That one goofy email created thousands of new customers. Whether it's a party or a package, you can turn a mundane moment into a Memorable Moment; you can give your customers something tangible to talk about. If you haven't done a good job with consistent Operational Excellence or haven't made any real connections to them through Personalized Service, these special experiences aren't going to make them love you. But if they already love you, a Memorable Moment will catalyze them to tell others to buy from you.

Hopefully, you have a good idea of what a Memorable Moment is. You may even have some ideas on what you could do for your customers. But before I wrap up, let me share with you the three moments my team and I have discovered to be especially effective as Memorable Moments.

If you want something to stick in their memory, it might help to understand a bit about how memory works. Let's take a little detour into neuroscience and look at how brains record memories.

The myth about memory is that we remember everything, that it's all stored in there somewhere, but we just can't retrieve all of it. The truth is that every night, when we sleep, our brains are deciding what to put into long-term memory and what to forget. We do not, in fact, remember everything. Even when we remember an experience, we don't enter all the details of that event in our memory. When you remember a great trip or even a great dinner, a few of the moments will rise to the surface while the rest of the moments fade into the background as a general experience. There is a predictable pattern to which moments our brains like to encode in long-term memory.

Specifically, there are three types of moments that our brains are hardwired to remember: beginnings, pain/pleasure spikes, and endings.[10]

First, beginnings matter. The first day at a new school or new job is vivid. The rest of the days will blur into a vague memory.

Second, research shows that you create Memorable Moments when you break the script or surprise customers with a strong physical sensation that gets locked into their memories. We are wired to notice changes in the world around us, to spot movement in the jungle, to remember which of these things is not like the other ones.[11]

Third, how something ends will have a huge impact on how we remember the entire experience. The last ten minutes of a movie can determine whether we like the entire film or not. Studies on painful medical procedures revealed that the last thirty seconds of a procedure have a big impact on the overall rating of the pain.[12] This effect is so strong that adding more time to the procedure to make the pain taper off gently actually results in better ratings, even though they have objectively experienced more pain. When the ending is less painful, the overall experience was remembered as less painful.

As you're planning where to experiment with your Memorable Moments, I recommend you work with the brain's bias rather than against it. Align your Memorable Moments with these moments in your customers' lives. I call these the "wet-cement moments," because a little bit of effort will make a lasting impression. Sure, you *can* make an impression on dry cement; it will just take a lot more work.

You can make your Memorable Moments personal or professional. Your customers can come away feeling like a great person, a great team, or a great company. Either approach works. You just have to fit the right feeling with the right customer.

STRONG STARTS

Since the first "wet-cement moment" is beginnings, you may want to consider designing a Strong Start to make a good first impression. If you own a restaurant, for example, make sure your staff is asking every single person, "Is this your first time dining with us?" If not, you can welcome them back or thank them for coming again. If it is their first time, then you should jump on that to make them feel extra special. Give them a treat, ideally a signature dish they can't get at any other restaurant. One of my favorite restaurants in Dallas, Texas, is The Rustic. Part of what makes it awesome is that when they discover you are a first-time guest, they give you a slice of their peanut butter pie. Not only is it really good pie but it stands ten inches high on the plate! Now that's a memorable slice of pie. I don't live in Dallas, but I have brought a lot of friends who live in Dallas to The Rustic for the first time, just so I can see their face when they bring out the peanut butter pie. (Well, also so I can help them eat the pie.)

The beginning could be a personal beginning in your customer's life, not about you. (Remember, they are the hero of the story.) Credit unions and consumer banks I've worked with realize they get visibility into a lot of the new beginnings of their customers' lives. They have learned to celebrate the purchase of a new home by sending gift baskets of critical household supplies, including chocolate chip cookies—a necessity, in my opinion.

A financial advisory company we've worked with throws epic baby showers for the grandchildren of their clients. Grandchildren are a very important new beginning in their clients' lives. Their financial advisor attends the shower and honors their client in front of their family, and they also set up an education fund for the new baby and put in the first $50, inviting anyone else who wants to contribute to the new baby's future success as well.

For years, Chick-fil-A has been hosting sleepover parties whenever a new store opens. Hundreds of people will camp in tents in the parking lot, playing games and making music, waiting to be one of the "First 100" to get in, earning a year of free Chick-fil-A meals in the process.

Remember Apple's memorable boxes? That's another way they're making the most of the new beginning—the beginning of their enjoyment of a new device. The high-end folio with your contract printed on heavyweight paper is another example of a Strong Start.

On the professional side, you can celebrate the launch of a new project in a memorable way. One electrical contractor we worked with started hosting the project kickoff for all the other subcontractors and the general contractor at a local brewery—and they scheduled the kickoff party for the end of the day on a Friday. The free beer they provided at the end of the meeting made for a memorable way to kick off the project.

Whenever you have a new beginning, you have an opportunity to create a Memorable Moment.

Don't just get started; start strong.

HERO MAKING

Most of us go through our days emotionally numbed by the predictability of the lives we live. Even when we do things well, the details blur together because they all have a similar "volume" in the music of our minds. One of the greatest gifts you can give your customers is to lift them out of their normal routine and help them feel like a hero for the things they're already doing.

Honor is one of the most powerful forces in the world. Men and women will die to protect their honor or the honor of their people. I don't just mean they did this in ancient times; people do this today, killing and dying to protect their honor. To increase status, even just for a few hours, people will spend significant amounts of time and money. If you can tap into even a small portion of this human drive, then you will activate a lot of storytelling that includes your company.

One of the more powerful ways to create a Memorable Moment is to make heroes out of your customers, to honor them publicly.

The first group of heroes I'd recommend you honor are your most engaged users. Reward behavior you want more of. This can be done through private moments like a formal ceremony or very efficiently through giving them a certificate via email. Sellers on eBay are given a public rank based on how many transactions they've done and how highly rated they are by their customers. Amazon calls out reviewers who have contributed the most and the best by giving them a special title and font when they leave a review. Microsoft, and many other software companies, hosts annual user meetings and spends some of that time to talk about their "best" customers, awarding plaques and trophies to those who engage the most.

One franchisee in the Chick-fil-A system ran a special program called "I Ate It All." He gave out a punch card with all the menu items listed on it and told his customers that if they ate at least one of each item by the end of the year he would give them a T-shirt (that said "I Ate It All at Chick-fil-A of Waynesboro") and talk about them online. There was no discount or any other special pricing. It was just a way to honor those who tried a lot of different types of food (they have a big menu for fast food, and most people just order their usual favorite).

If you think that sounds silly, you might be surprised at how many people put serious effort into this, ordering many items that they never had before and talking about their journey through the menu on their own social media pages. I have even been in a public event with this same franchisee when a person walked up and proudly introduced himself as a customer who successfully Ate It All in 2015.

Who are your best customers? How can you honor them?

Whatever you do, be careful not to make this into a rewards program that is just a discount for volume use (buy nine and get the tenth one free). This is about giving them public status. I'd rather you offer a special checkout line only for your best customers or a special color on their name badges.

Another option is to call out individuals who are doing wonderful things in the world, thanks in part to your help. These people might not be the largest clients you have, but they exemplify the purpose and values you want to embody. Tell their stories and show others that working with you is highly correlated with making the world a better place.

One company we have worked with for several years provides software for large health-care systems and statewide collections of doctors. When used right, their software helps doctors notice when a patient is trending worse (and maybe skipping prescriptions), so they can intervene before it gets too bad. They save a lot of heartache and money. To make heroes, the software company gives badges to the top 20 percent of doctors who get the best patient results. The award isn't about how much they do on the software, but it shows that the company is on the same noble mission—and it doesn't hurt that one of the best ways to get better patient outcomes is to use the software more.

When you shine the spotlight of honor on someone, you not only create a great experience that the individual wants to tell others about, but you also create a hero that others want to emulate. You are showing others the kinds of things they have to do in order to be honored themselves. It's important to give the same awards more than once—and to tell people that you are going to give the award again.

To take this to the next level, you can create unique awards to give them. Invent a category to highlight a specific situation, like "Best Patient Follow-Up Team," or to even create an inside joke, like "Most Dramatic Computer Crash of 2023." Better yet, give them a trophy that doesn't look like a normal trophy. I've seen clients use a giant mug and a wooden plank with words etched on them—and I've seen these unusual awards sitting in a client's office, displayed in a place of honor. Make it unique. Make it a Memorable Moment.

Another way of heightening these moments of honor is to take your clients to a new location. Get out of the regular office. Our brains are sensitive to our environment, and studies have shown that our memory of an event is stronger when there is a unique place associated with it.[13] The sounds, smells, and physical feeling of being in a new place create a rich experience for us all. Seeing a video of a waterfall is not the same as standing near the rushing water in person.

It might mean taking your client to lunch once a year. It might mean taking them even farther. For some of our client companies, we design and facilitate executive leadership development programs. At the beginning and end of these programs, we take them to Washington, DC, and Disney World. We could just tell the story of Martin Luther King Jr.'s "I Have a Dream" speech from a boardroom in Dallas, but we would rather stand on the steps of the Lincoln Memorial, on the very spot where he delivered that speech, and watch the video. The location turned it into a Memorable Moment.

But it doesn't have to be intense or expensive. You can do simple things like add music to the moment. Movies lean heavily on music for the emotions. Just try watching a movie on mute and see how it changes your experience. Or you can show up in person to honor someone. One of our yearlong projects included a mix of quarterly live sessions and monthly video meetings with our clients. The final session in the program was scheduled to be done virtually, but we surprised a client by showing up in person instead, with balloons and snacks.

That brings me to the power of food. People bond more deeply while eating together. This is true in all cultures and at all times. However, if you do bring food, spend the money to get something unique and high quality. The whole point is to create a Memorable Moment. Spending an extra $50 for the over-the-top experience is worth it. They won't tell stories about the generic sheet cake from Walmart. But they might take pictures in front of the chocolate fondue fountain.

NOSTALGIC CEREMONIES

Whenever something comes to a close, our emotions swell. Endings are bittersweet. We look back and get nostalgic. Simple things, like where we sat in a classroom thirty years ago, feel important to us. And we get excited—and nervous—about what comes next. Endings are naturally memorable. However, too many companies finish an engagement and walk away without even looking over their shoulder.

When I talk about endings, you might think, *I don't want endings! I want my customers to stay with me. Endings would be a bad thing.* That's fine. Remember that Memorable Moments is a small gear in your Customer Experience Engine. You don't need to do all of these. In fact, you *shouldn't* do all of these. It would be too much. It takes only one or two events per year to make them feel like a Jedi and tell others to work with you.

But some of us have natural work rhythms built around starting and finishing major projects. How we end these projects is important. If you have client relationships that go beyond a single transaction, then designing memorable endings is a big opportunity to get your customers talking about you.

This insight about endings can be applied in many different ways. At the end of a long project, throw a party. Even in short transactions, there are small things you can do. Many restaurants give you mints on the way out, no extra charge. The ending of a presentation should have some of your most emotional points. The final page of your tax report could be a thank-you note with a gift card taped to it. Don't just end your effort; finish with flair.

And even if all your customers keep working with you, they will experience endings in their personal life. If you have a strong system of providing Personalized Service, then you will learn about events in their life such as retirement, graduations, or even the death of a loved one. If you do learn about these endings, you can show up and make these moments memorable. They may never want to end their professional relationship with you because you showed up for them when something in their personal life ended.

A great example of this comes from Chewy.com, a company that sells pet supplies online, including subscriptions for food. Most pets have shorter life spans than humans, so owning a pet usually means we will have to lose them at some point. Rather than see this as just a drop in sales, Chewy sees this as a Memorable Moment for their customers.

This has a huge impact on their customers during a difficult time in their lives. For example, here is an online post from a Chewy customer:

"Sadly, we lost our family cat this week suddenly and I had to return an order from Chewy for a special food that we had ordered for him. They sent an email that brought tears to my eyes sending their condolences, giving me a refund and told me I could donate the food. Today we received flowers and the nicest note. In times like these, customer service and kindness matter so much, and I will be a forever customer of Chewy because of this."[14]

Having designed and hosted a lot of big ending ceremonies, I've learned a few things about how to make them great. Lean into the nostalgia. Sometimes leaders are afraid to honor the thing that just ended because they want to emphasize how the new thing is going to be better. But if you don't give people a chance to feel nostalgic about the "good old days," then they have a harder time letting go and moving on. It costs you nothing to acknowledge that there were some good things about that season. In fact, I think about this as a "funeral" for the season that ended. We honor the good parts, share memories, and mark the end of an era.

What this looks like depends on what has ended. I already mentioned the homebuilding company that rolls out the red carpet. That's a high-energy moment. But even in that largely future-focused experience, the company looks back and remembers by presenting the customer with a picture book of their construction process, from foundation to framing to final walk-through.

One of our clients is a hospice company that is growing crazy fast. They passed their ten-year stretch goal in four years and are still speeding up. It's a bit odd to say that a hospice company has raving fans, but they do. Part of why they're so loved is how they honor their patients after they have passed. They often collect stories that even the families didn't know and train their people on how to share them at the funerals. Other people see how they honor their late patients and think, *When it's time, I want my mom to be cared for like that.*

But it doesn't have to be a permanent ending. You can mark the end of a year or the end of a season. New Year's Eve is a big opportunity. The end of summer (and start of school) is a major moment in the lives of families with kids.

After learning about Memorable Moments, one of our clients, a Mexican restaurant in the United States, started hosting parties to watch the professional soccer games of the Mexican teams.

Many of their customers came to eat there because it reminded them of home, so this restaurant decided to help them connect with other aspects of Mexican culture. Also, consider the many bookstores that hosted Harry Potter parties when the books were released. Find something that is already important to your customers and throw a party for them to enjoy.

Bottom line: pay attention to the endings in your customers' lives. Whether it's the end of your project or the end of a personal situation, these moments are already going to be significant to them. Find a way to elevate these occasions into Memorable Moments that are associated with you.

THE POWER OF PICTURES

You have probably heard the saying, "A picture is worth a thousand words." Well, in modern times, I think a picture is worth ten thousand words. If you want to make a story go viral, you need a picture that people can share—and I'm not just talking about stories that are shared on social media. Haven't you been to a dinner when someone pulled out their phone and passed a picture around?

Whatever you do, find a way to take pictures. Don't hope that *someone else* will take pictures. If it's a major event, you might want to hire a professional photographer. But with the quality of cameras in our phones, you can probably just assign the task to someone on your team.

Then, send these pictures to your clients. Maybe you can add your logo to the bottom corner or put a caption or frame around it. If that's too hard, just send the picture right off your phone. You greatly increase the chances that your customers will share the story if you give them a picture to share.

QUESTIONS TO CONSIDER

✿ *What are your unique traits? Are you local or national?*

✿ *What's special about your story compared to your competitors?*

✿ *What kind of Jedi do your customers want to feel like?*

✿ *How do your customers feel about themselves after they buy from you?*

✿ *How could you celebrate the beginning of each customer relationship?*

✿ *What heroes do you want to honor? Superusers? Mission partners?*

✿ *Are there causes you could invite your customers to be a part of in partnership with you?*

✿ *How could you elevate your "box-opening" experience?*

✿ *How can you celebrate your customers in your project endings?*

✿ *What endings are happening in your customers' personal lives that you could elevate?*

CHAPTER NINE

HEALTHY
LEADERSHIP TEAM

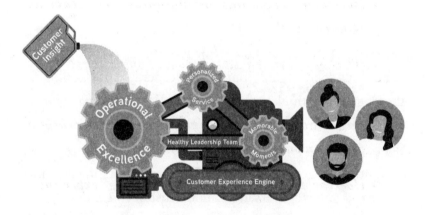

*T*he last system of the Customer Experience Engine is different from the others. On the diagram, Customer Insight is the fuel that pours into the engine, and three gears make up the heart of the engine. Operational Excellence is at least as big as the other two combined, which are Personalized Service and Memorable Moments.

Wrapped around these three gears, behind these major programs, is the "belt" of a *Healthy Leadership Team*.

This isn't something the customers see directly, but it is the system that keeps everything else in your engine running. It determines your pace of growth (how fast your engine turns) and ensures that all the other systems stay synced with each other.

Honestly, this belt didn't use to be in the diagram. I didn't include a Healthy Leadership Team at all in the first versions of the Customer Experience Engine. That's not because I don't think good leadership matters. I got my master's degree in business with a concentration in organizational leadership. I have designed leadership development programs in partnership with Harvard and Duke. I believe that good leadership is behind all good organizations, that leaders set the ceiling for the team. I even think leadership principles can change how we show up in our families, shaping the course of generations in dramatic ways.

But, back then, I didn't think I needed to get into all of that to have a good conversation about customer experience. *Of course* leadership matters! As one of my heroes, John Maxwell, says, "I think everything rises and falls on leadership." I have already written multiple leadership books. I wasn't planning to write another general leadership book. This book is supposed to be about customer experience, how legendary brands create raving fans. And I can't include everything that matters in life in this book. Being physically healthy matters too. If we don't take care of our bodies, then we don't have the energy to do great work, and we won't live long enough to enjoy the fruit of our efforts. Our spiritual lives matter. As Jesus said, "What does it profit a man to gain the whole world and forfeit his soul?" (Mark 8:36 ESV). While all these things matter, I wanted to focus this conversation on the topic at hand: customer experience.

However, after helping several companies create their own version of the Customer Experience Engine, I ran across the same problem again and again. When the leadership team wasn't healthy, the engine never came together and the company never created raving fans. Some of the work would happen, but none of the benefits came to pass. Whenever we worked on their leadership team, however, the engine started humming and the customers started raving.

I eventually changed the diagram to include the belt. It turns out that if you don't have a Healthy Leadership Team, you can't build a Customer Experience Engine. Even though I'm talking about this system last in this book, this is now actually one of the first things we work on when we partner with a company to build their own Customer Experience Engine.

Why? How does something so indirect have such a big impact on the customer experience?

As best as I can tell, there are two major reasons. First, if you want a great customer experience, you need to deliver a great employee experience. It's the frontline employee who directly serves customers. If they are fully engaged and equipped, then they will serve your customers with energy and excellence. As leaders, we might say our primary "customers" are our employees. If you don't have healthy leaders, then you can't have engaged employees. Our job is to set them up for success.

After years of helping companies with this, I also have documented how to make this happen with an *Employee Engagement Engine*, but that is a conversation for another book. For now, we'll just stick to how healthy leadership benefits your customers' experience with your business.

HEALTHY LEADERS

How do you become a healthy leader? How do you even know how healthy you are as a leader? There's more to say here than I can squeeze into a single chapter, but I don't want to move on without at least giving you a practical way to improve the health of your leadership and leadership team. The one thing I'd tell you is to use self-awareness tools.

Our health depends on our self-awareness; you can't improve something if you aren't aware that it needs improvement. It is our blind spots, the things we avoid at all costs, that ironically determine the shape of our culture. To increase health, start by increasing self-awareness. After decades of working on improving self-awareness for myself and my clients, I have come to see the power of using tools to spark these breakthroughs. What doesn't work so well is isolating yourself and trying to discover who you are on your own. Deep reflection is really powerful *after* you have some real-world feedback to think about. If you only listen to your own thoughts, you only get more certain about your existing ways of thinking. We need the outside perspective of others to help us notice new things and think new thoughts.

You can use tools like personality assessments, 360° feedback processes, and leadership coaches to provide new insights. Then, sort through all the data and choose something to improve. Not all of it will be accurate. That's okay; there is usually something valuable and actionable even in bad feedback.

I use these tools often, and I'm much better for it. In fact, I take a new personal assessment at least once a year. They aren't all equally awesome, but each one helps me think about how I show up in the world. Several times, I have used a 360° feedback process to get input from those above me, my peers, and those I lead. And even though I am a coach, I have my own executive coach I meet with once a month.

Health isn't a binary status, good or bad, it's a continuum from worse to better, and there's always room to grow. The healthier the individual leaders of your company are, the healthier your entire organization will be. Remember, everything rises and falls on leadership.

HEALTHY LEADERSHIP TEAM

If you want any of the benefits, you have to implement the whole engine. The first reason is about healthy individual leaders. You need your whole leadership team rowing the same direction. Just because you have healthy individuals doesn't mean they know how to work together as a healthy team. It's the difference between a track team and football team.

Growing up, I loved playing a lot of sports. For seven years in a row, I was on the football team in the fall and the track team in the spring. I thoroughly enjoyed both those teams and learned a lot. I could tell you story after story from those years. Unfortunately, something I can't tell you is our track team's win-loss record. I have no idea how good we were as a team. I don't even know if we won more than we lost. I have a vague recollection of the track meet results being announced on the loudspeaker, naming schools that got first, second, and third overall, but I don't remember where we showed up in that mix.

At this point, you could be excused for guessing that I'm not very competitive. You would be wrong, though. I love winning, and I love keeping score, even when it's not a formal sport. If anything, I might be a little too competitive.

For example, I can tell you our win-loss record for my football seasons. We had some dramatic ups and downs. For two years, the quarterback of my school's football team was Danny Kanell. If you're a football fan, you might recognize him as the quarterback for the FSU Seminoles in the early 1990s, an NFL quarterback for the Giants and the Falcons until the mid-2000s, and a sports commentator in the mid-2010s. Danny wasn't alone as a standout athlete in our little private school; his class had several players who went on to play for top college teams. Of course, we totally rode their coattails to the state championship two times, winning the first year and losing the next.

The reason I say we rode their coattails is because the next year, after Danny and his buddies graduated, we lost every single game until we went into the final game of the season with an 0–8 record, playing against the other worst team in our district, who also had an 0–8 record. In that final game, we played the hardest we had all season. One of us was going to be the worst team in the league, and it wasn't going to be us! With twenty-nine seconds to go, we were down by one point. Then, my brother (who was on the team with me) kicked a field goal that put us up by two. We knew they were bad enough that they couldn't score in the remaining time. We had won! We went crazy! All our players cleared the bench and ran onto the field, jumping onto each other in a giant pile and screaming at the top of our lungs. In fact, we celebrated so hard we accidentally dislocated the shoulder of one of our own players. Our coach was shouting for us to get off the field (the game wasn't actually over yet). And as silly as this sounds, that game was one of the most satisfying moments of my football career—securing our spot as *not* the worst team in the league.

So, I might be a little competitive. But if I'm that competitive, why can't I remember whether our track team won or not? It's not because I didn't care about winning; it's because of the way track teams keep score and reward athletes. You can earn points for each race. First-place runners get the most points, while second and third place earn fewer points for their school. At the end of the track meet, they add up all the races, and the school with the most points wins. I liked beating the other schools, but it didn't really impact me. See, you didn't go to the state championship as a team; you could earn a spot in the state meet only by winning your individual races. The top performers in each event moved on, going from the district meet to the regional meet and finally to the state meet.

Honestly, the reason I can't tell you the team score is because it didn't really matter to me.

Why am I telling you all this? Am I trying to relive my glory days as a high school athlete? Well, maybe. But it's also a useful analogy for leadership teams. You can call it a team, even have regular meetings, and add up all your efforts into an overall score. But none of that automatically makes you a true team, just like my track team wasn't a true team.

Many of the company leadership teams I've worked with were more like a track team than a football team. Your individual results determined whether you were rewarded. Sure, we added everyone's performance together to see the overall company results. But if an individual leader achieved their goals, then they weren't going to be bothered if something went wrong in another area of the company. When I was on the track team, I wanted my friends to win. I liked them as people, and I was glad to see them do well—but I didn't need them to win in order to win myself.

However, a football team is very different. Everyone has a different job to do. The wide receivers are measured very differently than the linebackers. There is no way for a player to win without the entire team winning. When I played football, I never had one of my coaches tell the offense that they won while making the defense run laps for losing us the game. We won or lost together. I got corrected (sometimes loudly) when I made mistakes. But it wasn't about me. They challenged me because it would impact the overall score. And when someone else dropped the ball, we all got involved because we needed him to play well.

Which one does your leadership team feel like—track or football?

Why does this matter for your Customer Experience Engine? Well, what we've found in helping companies make this happen is that if you don't run the whole engine, you don't get any of the benefits. Every system is essential, feeding off each other to create raving fans. Like a football team, you can't win the game if some of your leaders drop the ball. If you don't have Operational Excellence, you can't compensate with more Personalized Service. If you don't have Customer Insight systems in place, you will put on Memorable Moments that your customers don't care about. You can't yank out one of the engine's gears and expect to run. If your whole team runs the whole engine, the normal output is a raving fan. And if you implement 70–80 percent of the engine, you will get 0 percent of the results.

Like a real-life engine, you can't just yank out one system and expect the rest of the engine to work. You can expend 75 percent of the effort but get none of the benefit. So, don't pick your favorite section of this book and do only that. It won't work.

Without Customer Insight, you risk building an engine that successfully delivers an experience your customers don't want—or the market might change and you wouldn't notice. Many great brands have been lost because they lost sight of Customer Insight, from Blackberry to Blockbuster. Without Operational Excellence, your customers won't trust you, so nothing else you try to do for them will be credible. Without Personalized Service, you won't make the kind of connections that build bonds with your customers. And without Memorable

Moments, your customers might love you, but they won't tell anyone to buy from you, so you won't grow. Most of the engine delivers few of the results. But the *whole* engine delivers raving fans as the normal course of business.

You need everyone on your leadership team to buy in and build their part of the engine. If you try to build the Customer Experience Engine like a track team, it's not going to work. You need to approach this like a football team, with different positions all working together for a team win.

HEALTHY VS. SMART

Before I talk about how to build a Healthy Leadership Team, I want to warn you about what it's not. This isn't about how talented and smart your leaders are. Having smart leaders is a good thing. Smart leaders can handle more information and more tasks. Smart leaders can move faster. I'm pro-smart. But there is a world of difference between *smart* and *healthy*.

When we ask leadership teams how well they work together— how healthy they are—they sometimes tell us how smart they are. They usually don't use the word *smart*. They typically talk about their expertise and accomplishments. They share their strategic plans. All of that is good. I'm all for helping leaders get smarter. I mean, I just spent most of this book sharing stories and asking you questions so you can think more intelligently about your business. But if your team isn't healthy, it doesn't matter how smart you are.

Good decision-making is shaped more by how healthy you are than how smart you are.

Smart leadership teams who aren't healthy often compete with each other to have the best idea. Healthy leadership teams combine their ideas into a new and better idea. Smart-only leadership teams keep their best resources for their own projects. Healthy Leadership Teams share their best resources, swapping team members and even sharing budget dollars so the most important projects have a better chance to succeed. Smart-only leadership teams can't admit failures, and the members will distance themselves from any leader who gets caught dropping the ball. Healthy Leadership Teams discuss struggles early and collaborate to solve each other's problems. Smart-only leadership teams feel like they are taking a high-pressure, high-stakes test every time they meet. They are relieved to have survived another meeting. Healthy Leadership Teams often say the best part of their week is their team meeting. It's the most engaging, empowering, and productive thing they do. That's not exaggeration—that's literally what healthy teams in a wide range of industries have told me.

Frankly, the great majority of the leadership teams I have worked with had plenty of smart people. You don't get very far as a leader without real expertise in your field. I have seen a few incompetent individuals in leadership roles, but they usually don't last long.

However, the truth is that being smart enough to lead well is pretty common. Most companies have already solved for this problem. But many of the teams I have worked with weren't Healthy Leadership Teams—at least, not when we started working together. They all had the individual horsepower to do a good job, but they weren't all pulling the company in the same direction. You don't solve this problem by getting smarter. More horsepower doesn't get you better results. Ironically, without team health, all that extra intellectual horsepower creates more tension, not more progress.

If your team isn't what you would call healthy, don't get too discouraged here. It doesn't mean your individual leaders aren't healthy. Certainly, if you have a dishonest manipulator or an angry curmudgeon on your team, then it's going to be very hard to build a healthy team. But what I see more often is a group of individuals with good intentions who have not yet figured out how to work as a healthy team.

One of the interesting lessons from comparing my experiences on the track team and the football team is that while I had very different experiences in the spring and the fall, we had the same friends on both teams. Our football coach asked us to play another sport in the spring to stay in shape, and almost all of us chose track and field. On the football field, we were a cohesive unit who celebrated wins with intensity (maybe too much intensity sometimes). On the track, we didn't even notice when the other guys were racing, let alone care whether they won or lost.

We didn't go from good people to bad people every spring. The rules changed, not us. Our behavior was a product of the system we were in. When you change their environment, you change their behavior.

If you have a leader who simply will not collaborate, who insists on looking good by undermining others, it's possible that you may have to replace that leader when you try to become a

Healthy Leadership Team. But my guess is that you probably already have the right leaders; you just have an environment that rewards individual accomplishment rather than team wins.

You can design a different system. You don't have to play the way everyone else in your industry does. You get to decide what game you want to play. You can become a Healthy Leadership Team.

How to become a high-performance leadership team deserves a whole other book—and there are already some good books on that if you're interested. I'm not going to attempt to fully answer the question on how to build a Healthy Leadership Team. But I don't want to leave you with nothing, so I'm going to share two ways to assess how healthy your team is.

TRUST

Your team can only be as healthy as the level of trust you have with one another. And like health, trust is not an all-or-nothing quantity. It is a continuum, from low to high, with multiple factors combining to produce an overall feeling.

Trust is the operating system that teams run on. With low trust, our efficiency is low. We have to explain our thinking more, create extra rules to ensure high quality, check in more often to see if our employees and team members are complying with those rules, and even spend time doing things that protect our backsides but don't produce value for our staff or customers. The opposite of each of these is true when trust is high. Low trust is a tax on every interaction, while high trust is a boost.

By itself, trust is not enough to produce a high-capacity team. You will need to develop other team skills such as group decision-making, coach scorecards versus player scorecards, and learning together. But without trust, none of those other skills will make you a healthy team. Everything is built on the foundation of trust.

One of the first things to evaluate on your team is the level of trust that the team has.

FIVE LEVELS OF TRUST

Over the years, I developed a tool to help leadership teams evaluate and increase their trust, called the Five Levels of Trust:

The largest layer at the bottom, Level 1, is titled Knowledge. It might sound obvious, but all relationships begin with knowing things about each other, even if that is just a name or the company they work for or that their daughter is on the same soccer team as yours. It has to be shared knowledge. After all, you can't have a relationship of any kind unless you at least know each other exists! For example, I grew up watching Michael Jordan dominate basketball courts all over the world. I know a lot about him, but I don't know him personally. And, as far as I know, he doesn't know I'm alive. It doesn't matter how much information I know about him; if there isn't some *shared* information, then our trust level is at zero.

You can increase trust by sharing more information with each other. You may start with simple questions like, "Where did you go to school?" and progress to more information-rich questions like, "What did you major in at school?" and "How good were your grades?" The more you know, the better your chances of building trust. It's easier to build trust if you went to the same school. But even learning that they come from a very different background is meaningful and helps to develop trust.

As vital as it is, though, you can't build a high-trust relationship with knowledge alone. It's the lowest level of trust in our pyramid. However, it's also the easiest level of trust to achieve, and we all have plenty of people in our lives who would fall into this category. These are the many acquaintances that we know. There's something there; it's more than what Michael Jordan and I have, but it's not a close relationship, either.

Level 2 on the pyramid is labeled Experiences. To grow a stronger relationship, share experiences with each other. Again, having cool experiences on your own and telling your team about them doesn't do that much to build trust. (That's a Level 1 way of engaging—simply sharing knowledge with each other.) But if you share an *experience*, when you go through something together, you increase trust.

One universal example of this is sharing a meal together. In every culture, modern and ancient, people bond by eating together. The same conversation is elevated by the presence of tea or cookies. It's hardwired into us, so an easy way of growing the trust on your team is to bring food into more of your meetings. Of course, you can take them out to dinner too.

But it's not just food. There are a lot of trust-building experiences. The infamous trust fall is intended to serve this function, as is the white-water rafting trip some teams go on. But risky physical adventures aren't necessary to build team trust. There is a lot of value in low-risk activities, whether watching a movie or going on a road trip.

Having mutual history creates a sense of belonging, that we are in the same tribe. People open up and become a little more self-disclosing because everyone can relate back to a "remember when we ..." moment.

But I learned early in my work as a consultant that experiences, even grand experiences, don't result in high-trust relationships. Trust falls alone can't build high-trust teams; it just gets you to the second level of our pyramid.

At Level 3, you share Opinions. What school you went to is knowledge. Whether that education was worth what it cost or not is your opinion. In our diagram, Level 3 is smaller than Level 2 and much smaller than Level 1. This shows that there are fewer people who we share our opinions with. That's okay. It's natural and necessary, even.

Some opinions are fun and easy, but some of them can be fairly risky to share. If I ask you what you think the best movie is, it probably doesn't feel too risky to share. (The correct answer is *The Matrix*, by the way.) Even if you disagree with me (like my wife does), it's no big deal. But it could be a big deal if I ask for your opinion on a controversial political issue.

This does not mean you have to agree with everything the other person thinks in order to build Level 3 trust. That does make it easier, but Healthy Leadership Teams have to be able to discuss a lot of different opinions and still trust each other.

If you keep building trust, you move up the pyramid to Level 4, which is labeled Feelings. Instead of telling you that I think *The Matrix* is the best movie, I could tell you how that movie makes me feel. We're swimming in deep waters here, and the number of people with whom we mutually share how we feel is relatively small.

Sadly, many of us were never taught how to name our own feelings, let alone how to share them with other people. And many business leaders believe that the ideal business would be one without feelings. Even when we try to avoid them, though— or perhaps *especially* when we try to avoid them—our feelings have a big impact on how well we work.

This has been popularized with the term *emotional intelligence*, and there are a ton of great resources on this topic. I won't try to restate all of that here; I just want to point out that a lot of people have proved that these "soft" feelings have a big impact on "hard" results.

But this isn't the highest level of trust. Level 5, the very tip of the pyramid, happens when we share Successes and Failures. When we open up about our struggles and our losses, we are engaging at the highest level of trust. I have found that, in many cultures, it is equally risky to openly share your big successes. Saying you were awesome today or that you are really good at something might create as much negative blowback as saying that you failed.

Sadly, some people have no one in their life that they can fully engage with on Level 5. It is not easy, nor is it automatic. There have been seasons in my life when I didn't have a single relationship at this level of trust. But before I talk about how to use the Five Levels of Trust to improve your leadership team, let me make a personal plea. Whether or not you experience this at work, pursue this kind of friendship in your personal life. If you ever had someone like this, then even if they have moved to another state, call them up and go out of your way to keep that relationship in your life. It's worth the effort.

HOW TO USE THE FIVE LEVELS OF TRUST TO IMPROVE YOUR LEADERSHIP TEAM

That's the overview of the five levels. It's a good start, but the real value is in this next section. If that's truly how trust is built, then there are some practical things you can do to build a high-trust Healthy Leadership Team.

Go in Order

As your team is building trust, don't skip to the most intense, most vulnerable interactions. To make this feel natural, establish trust at each level before attempting the next. Each group needs to get comfortable at one level before trying to move to the next. If you jump to Level 5 right away, it will just be awkward for everyone. Once in a while, people have the special experience of going deep with someone else quickly. Within hours, you feel like you have a high-trust friend. As awesome as this is, it's not something you should expect a typical team to do. Don't even try to jump to Level 3 too quickly. Don't skip ahead. In the long run, the fastest path to high trust is to go in order.

Safety without Similarity

In order to move to a higher level of trust, people need to feel safe engaging at the lower level. The easiest way for us to feel safe is to interact with people who are similar to us. If you come from the same place, have the same beliefs, share the same personality, and like the same foods, then it requires little risk to share fully with each other. However, if your team feels safe only when everyone agrees, then you will end up with a lopsided team, one that slips into groupthink and suffers from big blind spots. In fact, if everyone on your leadership team is exactly the same, you probably shouldn't pay them all to be on the team—their input is redundant! The best teams include diverse thinkers who bounce ideas off each other and improve each other's decisions. In order to do that, you have to figure out how to establish safety without similarity. The goal is not to make your team similar; the goal is to make everyone feel safe, even while disagreeing.

Lowest Common Denominator

So far, I've been describing trust in ways that are mostly one-on-one. This works similarly for groups, but there is an extra factor: Your leadership team will interact at the lowest level of trust between any two members, not the average of the trust levels on the team. If there is one person in the room that we don't trust, then we all hold back. To be ready to move to the next level, you have to enable each member of your team to establish safety at that level *with every other member on the team.* The whole room has to be comfortable sharing their opinions before you have team trust at that level.

Higher Is Harder

It is easy to establish safety at Level 1. There is very little risk in most of the information we share, so you can move from Level 1 to Level 2 quickly. However, each time you move higher, it's harder to establish safety. It takes longer, and fewer people will be willing to engage. Not everyone will go to Level 5 with you. So, don't be misled by how quickly you progress in the early stages. If you want to go high, get ready to do a lot of hard work. This is why the diagram I chose for this is a pyramid. It's not practical to invest the time and energy going to Level 5 with everyone I meet. Based on logistics alone, we all have decreasing numbers of people we connect with as we climb the pyramid.

At Least Level 3

To be a Healthy Leadership Team, you don't have to get everyone to Level 5. As powerful as that is, it's also a lot of work. And everyone on the team has to be willing to get really vulnerable and invest a lot of time to forge what often become lifelong friendships. It's beautiful when this happens, but it's not necessary. In order to be a Healthy Leadership Team, you just need to reach Level 3, where you share opinions.

If you don't feel safe sharing your opinions, even when you disagree with others on your team, then you won't be able to improve your plans or avoid your problems. Therefore, be intentional about getting your team to Level 3 and then remain open for more without demanding more.

FINAL PRACTICAL TIP

After partnering with many organizations to help them build their Customer Experience Engine, my team and I have learned a lot on how this process works. It would require another book to unpack everything we've discovered, and I'm not going to attempt it here as we near the end of this book. There are other good resources on how to make lasting change in your organization. There is, however, one lesson I want to leave you with as you start building your own engine:

Building a Customer Experience Engine is not an event. It's more like baking a cake.

First, you need all the ingredients; you can't just use the sugar and flour. Even things you don't expect, like salt or baking soda, are essential. And you need to mix them together in the right sequence; the icing goes on after the cake is done cooking and has cooled a bit.

Second, while there may be a moment of inspiration, when you and your team buy into the vision, you don't design the systems and call it complete. To make this your new normal, you need to go through the process—and you need to sustain your effort for long enough. The good news is that you don't need to sprint. You can make real change through steady work. I have often heard Dan Cathy, chairman of Chick-fil-A, say the key to effecting changes as a leader is gentle pressure sustained over long periods of time. When you're baking a cake, you can't turn up the oven to 900° and bake the cake in seven minutes.

If you're starting from scratch, be prepared for two or three years of sustained effort before this becomes your new normal. We're talking about establishing new organizational habits. If you have ever been told it takes twenty-one days to build a habit, you were lied to. It's closer to twenty-one *weeks*—and that's just for an individual. Getting your entire organization to a whole new level (and keeping them there) requires steady marching in the same direction for a long time.

This is why I depict the Healthy Leadership Team as a belt rather than another gear. I wanted to communicate that the role of the leadership team is to get all the gears moving, to keep them synchronized, and to continually go through the loop, year after year. It's not a onetime event; it's a commitment to continuous improvement. It's not about the one idea that will change your customer experience; it's about becoming a team that continually upgrades your customer experience.

This is a lifestyle change, not a crash diet you endure for one month.

I'm not sharing this to discourage you. Quite the opposite. I've seen this change happen many, many times. I'm sharing this final tip so you don't have unrealistic expectations, so that you will be fully prepared for the *entire* journey and not quit six months into the process.

This journey is possible. Many others have traveled this road, and with the right equipment in your backpack, you can do it too. This isn't magic. It's just a set of systems that, when executed, deliver a reliable result.

QUESTIONS TO CONSIDER

✿ *How healthy are the individual leaders on your team?*

✿ *Is there a leader that is not a good team player but you tolerate because they get results?*

✿ *Does your leadership team operate more like a track team or a football team?*

✿ *What are the benefits of a track team approach?*

✿ *When would a track team approach be more appropriate than trying to make a group operate like a true team?*

✿ *What are the benefits of a football team approach?*

✿ *What parts of your organization would benefit from being more like a football team?*

✿ *At what level of trust (Level 1–5) does your team operate?*

✿ *What could you do to advance to the next level of trust with your team?*

✿ *Is there a person who is holding the rest of the team back? What could you do to grow that person so they don't negatively affect the operation of the team?*

CHAPTER TEN

WHY BUILD A RAVING FAN ENGINE?

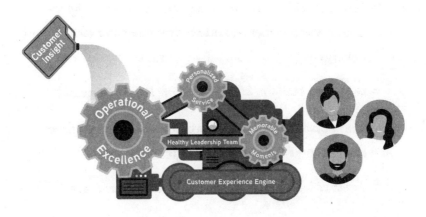

I've spent the entire book talking about how to build a raving fan engine, but I can't finish without talking for just a little bit about why. If you aren't clear on why you want to build this engine, it's going to be much harder to stay the course and be successful.

REALITY CHECK

Let's be honest: it takes more work to build and run a raving fan engine than it does to build a regular company with "satisfied" customers. If you've gotten this far and have only written down a couple of cool marketing ideas you can implement next quarter, then you might have missed the core of this book. If you paste some Memorable Moments on top of your old systems, you will not create raving fans. To build a profitable engine, you might need to overhaul your operations, hire different people, and even create new departments. It may require change after change, for year after year.

Change requires energy, and you're going to have to pour a lot of energy into your company for quite a while. You can't overhaul your systems or your habits overnight. And even when your engine is fully operational, it will still take a little while for your customers to adjust their opinion of you. Most people won't change their mind after a single new data point. They will need to see a pattern of good experiences before they start acting like raving fans.

The Customer Experience Engine isn't a shortcut, with tools to trick people into liking you. No, you're going to have to *earn* your raving fans.

(Sorry to be a bit of a downer, but I did tell you this book wasn't a motivational speech, right?)

If you want to make it to the other side of this change journey, you must get clear on why you're doing this before you get started. You will be paying a big price; what is the reward that you are doing it for?

> Only when you know your "why" will you find the
> courage to take the risks needed to get ahead, stay
> motivated when the chips are down, and move your
> life onto an entirely new, more challenging, and
> more rewarding trajectory. —Margie Warrell[15]

There are a lot of potential motivations for doing this. What's driving you?

RESPECT

Maybe you want to be the best in your industry. Maybe you want to earn the respect of your peers or even just earn your own self-respect when you look in the mirror. One of the worst regrets is knowing you could have been great at something . . . if you had only tried. Living up to your full potential is an honorable motivation.

If this strikes a deep chord in your heart, then name it and own it. What will it look like when you earn this respect? How will you know when you've made it to the next level? What will people do or say differently?

PROFIT

Maybe you see the long-term investment value in this strategy. One of the most important numbers in your business is the lifetime value of a customer. Let's be honest, it costs more to create a raving fan than it does to capture a satisfied customer. Sometimes a *lot* more. But that's only half the equation. The lifetime value of a raving fan is far, far higher than the value of a satisfied customer. You may invest more than your competitors, but you'll also earn much more than your competitors.

Plus, the exponential growth that comes from a base of raving fans talking about you is really powerful. Each year, you will gain more and more from your engine. I've been behind the scenes on many of the biggest brands with raving fans, and let me tell you that it is very profitable to have a Customer Experience Engine.

This has been validated again and again. A study by Frederick Reichheld of Bain & Company, published in *Harvard Business Review*, revealed that on average, it costs at least 600 percent more to acquire a new customer than it does to retain an existing customer (in some industries, it was over 700 percent). And the same study shared that increasing customer retention rates resulted in a profit increase of 25–95 percent.[16]

Also, a CEB Marketing Leadership Council survey reported that raving fans, on average, spend 31 percent more with a vendor they love than merely satisfied customers, and raving fans are 50 percent more likely to try a new product/service than merely satisfied customers.[17]

Bottom line: raving fans are really, really profitable.

If this is a major goal of yours, then get crystal clear on what success looks like. How much profit do you want to make by when? You can use the three differentiators of raving fans to make some real calculations. Remember, raving fans

1. buy more, more often
2. pay full price
3. tell others to buy from you

How much more will they buy than your typical customer today? At what price will you sell it to them? And, with those numbers in mind, how many raving fans do you need to reach your profit goals?

Exactly how valuable are raving fans to you? How much would you invest to make your goal come true?

STABILITY

Jack Welch, one of the most successful CEOs of the twentieth century, said, "When you're number four or five in a market, when number one sneezes, you get pneumonia. When you're number one, you control your destiny."[18] You may be in the same category as your competitors, according to the government survey, but if you have raving fans and they only have satisfied customers, you really aren't playing the same game they are.

I've been in meetings with many executive teams of major companies during massive recessions, from the dot-com crash of 2000 to the COVID-19 pandemic, and companies with Customer Experience Engines seem to live in a different reality. I heard one multibillionaire executive say, with a relieved shrug and a wry grin, "We have decided not to participate in this recession." When money is tight, their customers reduce spending everywhere else but with them. What they sell has become a part of their customers' identity, so they don't walk away quickly.

I'm not saying you're guaranteed success—very few things in this life are guaranteed. But you can face the same ups and downs as everyone else with a totally different set of tools. Raving fans stack the deck in your favor.

POSITIVE INFLUENCE

While all these motivations are valid, this last one might be my favorite. It is what motivates me. In addition to more respect, more profits, and more stability, a Customer Experience Engine allows you to have a significant positive influence on the world.

Think about it: if you get to know what your customers really want, become someone they can count on, make a personal connection, and help them feel like heroes, what you're doing is making their lives better. Yes, you'll make good money, but you'll also be making the world a better place.

You don't have to build a business that extracts money from people. You can build an engine that adds good to the world, that profits from making others' lives better. When you get this engine going, the more lives you improve, the more money you make. I don't know about you, but I get pretty excited about that kind of math.

After decades of working inside legendary brands, helping build some of the greatest brands of our time, I have learned a great deal. By far, the best lesson I have learned is this: There is no conflict between the noble path and the profitable path. In the short term, it sometimes looks like you need to choose between the two. But if you lift your head and look far enough down the road, you realize that the noble path is also the profitable path.

You don't have to choose between being good and being successful. You can build an engine that does both.

What if you had a core group of customers who were raving fans, who bought everything you made and recruited more raving fans for you? What if your staff was proud to be associated with you and your company? What if your customers went out of their way to spend more with you? And what if you didn't worry much about the rise and fall of the economy?

What would your life be like if you had a Customer Experience Engine?

You don't have to settle for satisfied customers. You don't have to wonder what might have been. You can become a legend in your industry. You can make good money by doing good in the world. Greatness is possible. Greatness is within your grasp.

All you need is the right engine.

WHAT TO DO NEXT

*B*y now, I hope you have a list of ideas for upgrading your customer experience, but you might be wondering which one to do first. I've been through this journey with a lot of companies, and I've learned a lot about the process of company transformation. Let me share the sequence that I usually follow.

First, start with the low hanging fruit. On your list, there might be some easy wins. There might be a few options that you know exactly how to do, have the resources to do, and know it won't take long to implement. Do those first.

Second, don't do any of the other items on your list yet. Before you spend time and money on them, do an assessment of your current customer experience. Don't assume you know what's going on because you've been working with your customers for years. Unless you've recently gone through a formal process to evaluate your customer experience, it's highly likely you're missing critical details. Before you invest time and money to make changes, get really clear on your current state.

All smart strategic planning is like getting directions from Google Maps. Not only do you need to know where you want to go, you need to know exactly where you are. Only then can you map out the fastest path to your destination.

ACKNOWLEDGMENTS

If I have seen a little further than others,
it is by standing on the shoulders of giants.
—Isaac Newton

While this book is built on what I have learned from working more than twenty years inside the engines of some truly great brands, I had a lot of help along the way. None of this would have been possible without many mentors pouring into me, including my parents, Fred and Bonnie Wozniak, who are not only great parents but brilliant professional mentors as well.

Other mentors whose wisdom found its way into this book include military leaders like Sean Moulton; ministry leaders like Alan Winter and Keith Chancey; artistic leaders like Scott Holesclaw, Jon Secrest, and Glenda Secrest; and business leaders like Ken Eldred, Phil Orazi, Mark Miller, Dan Cathy, and Truett Cathy.

Frankly, the influence my mentors had on me goes far beyond business insights. I wouldn't be the man I am without their personal investment in me. I have ridden on the shoulders of giants, men and women who changed my life through sharing their giftedness and inspiring me with their goodness.

In this book, I synthesized what my mentors taught me and added my own two cents. In some ways, this is my attempt to pass on what they taught me. Of course, much of what they passed on to me they learned from their mentors before them. This is a chain of wisdom, reaching back for centuries. And I hope some of what I shared in this book is worth you passing on to those you mentor.

Good artists copy, great artists steal. —Steve Jobs, who was actually quoting Pablo Picasso. But Picasso "borrowed" this quote from William Faulkner, who copied it from a work by T. S. Eliot.

ABOUT THE AUTHOR

Scott Wozniak, CEO of Swoz Consulting, has consulted with leaders on six continents, including Silicon Valley start-ups, family enterprises, and Fortune 500 companies. Scott is a member of Mensa (international genius society), reads over two hundred books each year, and has written four books.

He earned a master's degree in business with an emphasis in organizational leadership and has worked with some of the leading brands of our time, including multiple Silicon Valley "unicorns" and Nucor Steel. He also spent eight years as an employee at the Chick-fil-A headquarters, working directly with the founding family and executive team to design leadership development programs, set strategy, and lead company-wide upgrades—and though he is not an employee there anymore, he regularly consults with their leaders.

Before becoming a business consultant, Scott worked in nonprofits, primarily with children through sports camps, inner-city programs, and a national tour of stadium-filling conferences, complete with rock bands and comedians.

Before all of that, Scott was on stages all over the United States for eighteen years as a child actor (including a Christmas special on NBC) and an internationally touring singer in two choirs.

Scott lives in Atlanta with his wife and four children. In his spare time, he continues to write music, design board games, serve in local nonprofits, and push his boundaries through a variety of extreme sports, from heli-skiing to kitesurfing.

If you want to hear more of Scott's ideas, you can check out the other books he has written, listen to the podcasts he hosts, and sign up for his weekly newsletter. You can find links for all of that (and more) at www.ScottWozniak.com.

And if you want help building your own Customer Experience Engine, visit www.SwozConsulting.com. There you can learn about options for online programs, leadership coaching, and in-depth custom consulting projects. We have been accelerating the growth of companies for decades, so if you want to get there faster, we can help. We will add jet fuel to your campfire.

NOTES

1   Giovanni Bruno, "McDonald's Rethinks Its $2 Billion Ad Budget," The Street, October 26, 2017, https://www.thestreet.com/investing/stocks/mcdonald-s-to-examine-how-its-spending-its-ad-dollars-14362329.

2   Jessica Wohl, "McDonald's Puts Local Creative Accounts in Review, Aiming to Cut Dozens of Shops," Ad Age, July 12, 2017, https://adage.com/article/cmo-strategy/mcdonald-s/309726.

3   Caitlin Johnson, "Cutting through Advertising Clutter," CBS News, September 17, 2006, https://www.cbsnews.com/news/cutting-through-advertising-clutter/.

4   Clayton Christensen, *Competing against Luck: The Story of Innovation and Customer Choice* (New York: Harper Business, 2016).

5   Brian Taylor, "Nucor to Add Furnace Capacity to Arizona," *Recycling Today*, August 3, 2022, https://www.recyclingtoday.com/news/nucor-steel-recycling-melt-shop-kingman-arizona/.

6   Ken Silverstein, "Nucor Boasts Superior Greenhouse Gas Reductions for Steel Operations," Environment Energy Leader, September 27, 2022, https://www.environmentalleader.com/2022/09/nucor-boasts-superior-greenhouse-gas-reductions-for-steel-operations/.

7   Lewis Howes, "10 Lessons for Entrepreneurs from Coach John Wooden," *Forbes*, October 19, 2012, https://www.forbes.com/sites/lewishowes/2012/10/19/10-lessons-for-entrepreneurs-from-coach-john-wooden/?sh=294407bb16d5.

8   DevCookHouse, "Google Assistant Haircut Appointment Call," YouTube, May 8, 2018, https://www.youtube.com/watch?v=yDI5oVn0RgM.

9   Derek Sivers, "The Most Successful Email I Ever Wrote," July 17, 2011, https://sive.rs/cdbe.

10 Murray Glanzer and Anita R. Cunitz, "Two Storage Mechanisms in Free Recall," *Journal of Verbal Learning and Verbal Behavior* 5, no. 4 (1966): 351–60.

11 Chip Heath and Dan Heath, *The Power of Moments: Why Certain Experiences Have Extraordinary Impact* (New York: Simon & Schuster, 2017).

12 Dan Ariely, *The Upside of Irrationality: The Unexpected Benefits of Defying Logic* (New York: Harper Perennial, 2011).

13 Robinson Meyer, "In the Brain, Memories Are Inextricably Tied to Place," *The Atlantic*, August 12, 2014, https://www.theatlantic.com/technology/archive/2014/08/in-the-brain-memories-are-inextricably-tied-to-place/375969/.

14 See Jennifer Brookshire's post on LinkedIn: https://www.linkedin.com/feed/update/urn:li:activity:6844688284342472704/.

15 Margie Warrell, "Do You Know Your 'Why?' 4 Questions to Find Your Purpose," *Forbes*, October 30, 2013, https://www.forbes.com/sites/margiewarrell/2013/10/30/know-your-why-4-questions-to-tap-the-power-of-purpose/?sh=471a6f5373ad.

16 Amy Gallo, "The Value of Keeping the Right Customers," *Harvard Business Review*, October 29, 2014, https://hbr.org/2014/10/the-value-of-keeping-the-right-customers.

17 "17 Must-Know Lead Generation Stats for B2B Marketers," FusionGrove, October 20, 2017, https://fusiongrove.com/uploads/102017/Must_Know_Stats_for_B2B_Lead_Generation_Infographic.pdf.

18 "25 Lessons from Jack Welch," Deccan Group, May 20, 2011, https://deccangroup.wordpress.com/2011/05/20/25-lessons-from-jack-welch/.